Glorious REFRAINS

A Collection of Classic Hymns That Touch the Heart

featuring the artwork of

THOMAS KINKADE
Painter of Light™

NELSON BIBLES

Nashville

www.ThomasNelson.com

GLORIOUS REFRAINS

Scripture portions are from the New King James Version of the Bible
Copyright © 1982 by Thomas Nelson, Inc.

Reflections written and edited by Thomas Kinkade
and Jennifer Morgan Gerelds

Hymn stories written by Linda Taylor

Cover Design by Koechel Peterson & Associates, Inc.
Minneapolis, Minnesota

Interior Design and Composition by Que-Net Media™
Schaumburg, Illinois

Glorious REFRAINS

Presented to

Given by

Date

to Commemorate

Cherished Loved Ones We Remember

Name _____

Birthday _____

Birthplace _____

What they liked to do _____

_____

_____

Why they are so special to us _____

_____

_____

Name _____

Birthday _____

Birthplace _____

What they liked to do _____

_____

_____

Why they are so special to us _____

_____

_____

Name _____

Birthday _____

Birthplace _____

What they liked to do _____

_____

_____

Why they are so special to us _____

_____

_____

Name _____

Birthday _____

Birthplace _____

What they liked to do _____

_____

_____

Why they are so special to us _____

_____

_____

Treasured Family Memories and Traditions

Holidays:
(Christmas, Easter, Thanksgiving, faith celebrations...)

_____
_____
_____
_____
_____
_____
_____
_____

Vacations:
(Summertime fun, winter adventures...)

_____
_____
_____
_____
_____
_____
_____

Favorite Games and Entertainment:
(Music, sports, theater...)

_____
_____
_____
_____
_____
_____

Special Family Foods and Recipes:
(Foods and kitchen scents we remember with love)

_____
_____
_____
_____
_____
_____
_____
_____

Special Church Moments and Ceremonies

Name _____

Event _____

Date _____

How it was special _____

_____

_____

Name _____

Event _____

Date _____

How it was special _____

_____

_____

Name _____

Event _____

Date _____

How it was special _____

_____

_____

Name _____

Event _____

Date _____

How it was special _____

_____

_____

Name _____

Event _____

Date _____

How it was special _____

_____

_____

Name _____

Event _____

Date _____

How it was special _____

_____

_____

Name _____

Event _____

Date _____

How it was special _____

_____

_____

Name _____

Event _____

Date _____

How it was special _____

_____

_____

Happy Memories Captured in Time

photo

photo

photo

photo

photo

Glorious REFRAINS

12 | ASPEN CHAPEL

Amazing Grace

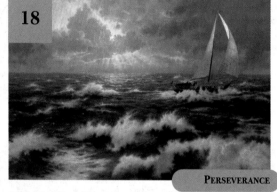

18 | PERSEVERANCE

It Is Well with My Soul

24 | END OF A PERFECT DAY

A Mighty Fortress

30 | POOLS OF SERENITY

Sweet Hour of Prayer

36 | GOOD SHEPARD'S COTTAGE

I Need Thee Every Hour

42 | A NEW DAY DAWNING

O for a Thousand Tongues to Sing

CONTENTS

REFLECTIONS FROM

A SACRED PLACE

Dear Friends,

There is a place in our souls that words alone cannot touch. A place where the deeper issues of life are understood, where our spirits meet God's in an incredibly emotional and profoundly real way. It can be found simply by communing with the Creator through nature. Other times honest, unpretentious prayer places us bare, but comforted before His throne. But one of the quickest, surest ways to transport our souls from the scorching winds of this world into the shade of God's love is through the beautiful experience of hearing and singing classic hymns.

For this reason, I keep an old hymnal by my bedside. I have found it to be an endless source of inspiration for my work; some of my pieces have even been titled after the name of a hymn. It is an incredible blessing to draw on the wisdom, experience, and strength of saints who have gone before us— those who have traveled down the road where we now walk, those who have felt the Father's faithful hand safely guiding them.

Don't get me wrong. I like contemporary music, too, and the simple phraseology

THOMAS KINKADE

and freedom of contemporary worship has a unique role in the Christian experience. But there's just something about the old hymns—almost all were born out of the direst circumstances. The inner pleadings of their helpless, hopeless souls—so similar to my own—give me renewed hope as they point me to Christ, the source of hope and strength. Hymns are the universal cry of Christians to Abba, our heavenly Father, who remains as stalwart and strong for us today as He was for those Christians centuries ago.

I guess I see hymns in much the same way as I view art. Those solid images of the gospel of grace—the visual and auditory sense of walking and talking with Jesus—provide tangible handles for understanding God's love. In a way, that's what my whole mission and calling as an artist is: to provide those same kinds of physical guide-rails that lead people to Christ. Hymns accomplish it through music (a spiritual medium in itself) and words of eternal truth. I paint the pictures that I pray will point people through color and imagery to the hope I have found in Christ. It is a uniquely universal medium—transcending any language

barrier—that reaches past the mind to the heart, where the work of God begins.

It is my pleasure to bring you *Glorious Refrains*, a compilation of history, thoughts, visual delights, and auditory sensations that are designed to set your soul free to sing the praises of our incredible Savior. Together with all the other saints in heaven and on earth, you can declare our Maker's praise as you discover that sacred place of love, peace, and hope God has reserved for you now and in the future. If it's like this now, I can't even imagine what it will be like in heaven. May Jesus Christ be praised!

Blessings,

Thomas Kinkade

Amazing Grace

Amazing grace, how sweet the sound,
That saved a wretch like me!
I once was lost, but now am found,
Was blind, but now I see.

John Newton
1725-1807

REFLECTIONS

from Thomas Kinkade

Even as a young boy, I had a sense that God loved me. The view was distorted, however, by the stringent system of faith my home church enforced on its followers. Like so many religious institutions, my church had inadvertently marred the beautiful message of God's grace by attempting to manufacture the righteousness only God can give. We were even compelled to sign a "pledge of behavior," where we promised to not sin in a particular way. Sure enough, as soon as I would sign my name, that very temptation would raise its ugly head and reconfirm in my mind my inability to live up to God's holiness.

What a relief it was for me to discover grace later in life. God's love was not a precarious emotion I could turn on or off by my successes or failures. His commitment was constant, even when mine was not. His love was powerful and permanent—I imagine much like the unwavering devotion my mother demonstrated to me. She is my best earthly example of unconditional love, helping me have a glimpse of what goes on in God's heart.

A SONG OF TENDER MERCIES

Grace is an intensely personal experience that happens at the core of the soul, where Christ meets with us one on one to revolutionize the way we view life. We can sing about it, define it, and talk about it all we want, but until we experience it in the deepest recesses of our hearts and minds and realize its all-encompassing power over our lives, we won't really understand it. For when God opens our eyes to our utter dependence on His love and compassion, we are suddenly released to love others in the same dynamic way. With no strings attached except to our loving Father, we can forgive, serve, and shower tender mercies on all those around us who also desperately need to know the wonderful embrace of God's amazing grace.

Amazing grace! how sweet the sound,
That saved a wretch like me!
I once was lost, but now am found,
Was blind, but now I see.

Grace is indeed amazing. It transforms sinners into saints; it overcomes the power of sin and sets people free. Grace is undeserved favor. When sinners come to Christ, they are given the free gift of God's grace. No matter how much we have sinned or how far we may be from God, He graciously accepts our repentance and enters our hearts and lives with the light of His salvation.

John Newton understood how amazing God's grace really is—so amazing that it was beyond his comprehension and beyond his ability to repay. God's grace stepped into John Newton's debauched life and transformed him. Newton knew that he was indeed a "lost, blind wretch," but God "found" him and helped him to "see" His amazing grace.

Born in London on July 24, 1725, John Newton was the son of a commander of a merchant ship on the Mediterranean. His mother died when he was a child, and, at the age of eleven, John went to sea with his father. After his father retired, John served on a man-of-war and eventually on a slave ship. In 1748 he became captain of his own slave ship, capturing people in Western Africa and taking them to slave markets in the West Indies and America. From these early years came Newton's description of himself as a "wretch." Yet God's amazing grace was not too far from this brutal man, for God had a plan for him.

'Twas grace that taught my heart to fear,
And grace my fears relieved;

How precious did that grace appear
The hour I first believed.

Grace is a precious gift—available to us only through the blood of Christ. Jesus paid the price; we need only accept the gift. Newton did just that.

On March 10, 1748, on a voyage back to England from Africa, this experienced sailor found himself facing a violent storm at sea that threatened to sink his ship. After struggling to keep the ship afloat and eventually getting through the storm safely, Newton remembered the words of desperation he had cried out from the ship, "Lord, have mercy on us." His safe arrival caused him to wonder at the grace of a God who would protect him. At that time, Newton began reading *The Imitation of Christ* by Thomas à Kempis. The message of God's grace through the storm and the words of that little book led John Newton to surrender his life to Christ on May 10, 1748. He had already seen a lot of life by the age of twenty-two and had known a lot of fear. Even God's grace must have at first seemed fearsome to Newton—for how could free grace possibly cover his many sins? But God's precious grace relieved his fears.

Through many dangers, toils, and snares,
I have already come;
'Tis grace hath brought me safe thus far,
And grace will lead me home.

The sailor and slave trader had plied the seas for many years. "Dangers, toils, and snares" had been a way of life for one engaged in such an occupation. Yet God had a plan for John Newton and had touched his life right there on the slave ship. Newton sensed God's grace in his life, bringing him safely through so much even during his wretched days far from God, and he knew that the same grace would bring him safely to his future home in heaven.

The touch of grace asks only to be accepted, but once accepted, brings great changes into people's lives. Newton continued in his slave trading for a time, however he attempted to bring humane conditions to the slaves on his ship. But God continued working in Newton's heart, and by 1755, he gave up slave trading and seafaring altogether. As one who truly knew the heartbreak and brutality of the slave trade, Newton became an effective voice against it.

After ending his career on the seas, Newton worked for five years as surveyor of tides in Liverpool. While there, he was influenced by the evangelist George Whitefield, as well as by John and Charles Wesley. This young man who had stopped going to school at age eleven began to educate himself—studying Latin, Greek, and Hebrew.

Newton decided to become a minister. In 1764, at age thirty-nine, Newton was ordained in the Anglican church and began his first pastorate in Olney, England (near Cambridge). Newton was a popular preacher, holding weekly services and prayer meetings, as well as touring to various parts of England to preach.

When William Cowper, a well-known writer of classical literature, came to live in Olney in 1767, he and Newton became friends. Newton desired new kinds of hymns to be sung at his services, and, when he couldn't find enough available hymns, he and Cowper decided to write their own. In 1779, the first edition of *Olney Hymns* was published—including 349 hymns, 280 of them written by Newton. This hymn of God's amazing grace appeared in this first edition under a different title.

The Lord has promised good to me,
His word my hope secures;
He will my shield and portion be
As long as life endures.

Newton lived out God's grace through the rest of his life. He never forgot the story of his early life and how God's grace had transformed him. Wherever he preached, large crowds would gather to hear the story of this former slave trader who had been set free by God's amazing grace.

After ending his ministry in Olney, Newton pastored in the St. Mary Woolnoth Church in London. He continued his work to abolish the slave trade through his relationships with influential politicians such as William Wilberforce. The year Newton died, 1807, was the very year that Parliament abolished slavery throughout its country and colonies.

When we've been there ten thousand years,
Bright shining as the sun,
We've no less days to sing God's praise
Than when we first begun.

Grace. We do not deserve it; we cannot earn it. God's grace is totally and absolutely free. We will never be asked to pay it back— we couldn't if we tried. This is difficult for us to accept. We want to pay God back, we want to deserve His favor, and we don't like taking a gift if we feel that we don't deserve it. Grace is a free gift given by God to undeserving people like you and me. Why did He do it? Because He is love. How did He do it? He paid the price demanded for our sin. God is just; He did not set aside His justice in order to offer us this grace. Jesus' death handled the deserved punishment for our sin so that God, in His grace, could offer us forgiveness.

That's what is so amazing about God's grace.

and grac

For there is no difference; for all have sinned and fall short of the glory of God, being justified freely by His grace through the redemption that is in Christ Jesus. ROMANS 3:22–24

Therefore, having been justified by faith, we have peace with God through our Lord Jesus Christ, through whom also we have access by faith into this grace in which we stand, and rejoice in hope of the glory of God. ROMANS 5:1, 2

For by grace you have been saved through faith, and that not of yourselves; it is the gift of God, not of works, lest anyone should boast. EPHESIANS 2:8, 9

Let us therefore come boldly to the throne of grace, that we may obtain mercy and find grace to help in time of need. HEBREWS 4:16

Through many dangers, toils, and snares, I have already come; 'tis grace hath brought me safe thus far, and grace will lead me home.

Gracious God,

Thank You for the gift of Your amazing grace. You allow me, a sinner, to come close to You because of Your grace. You sent Your Son to die on the cross for sinners because of Your grace. You offer me salvation because of Your grace. May I never take Your grace for granted. May I always remember that while it costs me nothing, it cost You everything. Thank You for saving me. Thank You for bringing me safe thus far; I know that Your grace will one day lead me safely home to You where I can sing Your praises forever.

Amen.

It Is Well with My Soul

Horatio G. Spafford, 1828-1888

1. When peace, like a
2. Though Sa-tan sho
3. My sin oh,
4. And, Lord, hast

It Is Well with My Soul

My sin—O the bliss of this glorious thought,

My sin, not in part, but the whole,

Is nailed to the cross, and I be

Praise the Lord, praise the Lord, O my soul!

Horatio G. Spafford
1828-1888

REFLECTIONS

from Thomas Kinkade

Life isn't always sunny. In fact, when storm clouds roll in they can be dark, low, and very menacing. Winds of unwanted circumstance buffet our souls as we lose sight of the light and seek desperately for some surer footing before the rain ransacks our hope completely. In the midst of life's storms, it is easy to feel lost. To lose hope. It's the common tendency of all, even Christians.

But the blessed truth is that Jesus knows. He cares. He even warned us that difficult times would come. And He also promised that He would never leave us nor forsake us. Furthermore, He fashions every event—even the most painful—into our good. He gives us these promises to anchor our souls, even in the most turbulent times.

In the painting, *Perseverance*, I utilize sources of light to convey that sense of hope—to illustrate the struggle to see beyond the darkness to the light. While the waves are great, the Creator of the waves—and calm—is greater still. Keeping our eyes focused on Him, even while we can't see Him, is the ultimate key to hope.

We must remember that no matter how dark the storm, the clouds and rain will pass. If we rely on Him, He will give us the strength to ride it out until the gray is pierced with His glorious light. It is always there, only hidden at the time. Soon it will shine brightly again as the warmth of His love leads us safely home.

BEYOND THE DARKNESS

When peace, like a river, attendeth my way,
When sorrows like sea billows roll;
Whatever my lot, Thou hast taught me to say,
It is well, it is well with my soul.

Though Satan should buffet,
Though trials should come,
Let this blest assurance control,
That Christ hath regarded my helpless estate,
And hath shed His own blood for my soul.

Sorrows like sea billows. Who among us has not, at times, felt the overwhelming sense of helplessness in the middle of pain, sorrow, worry, or trouble? When suffering comes, we feel as though someone has tossed us into an angry ocean, and we are left to the whims of the sea billows as they toss us about and crash over us. Helpless. Needing rescue lest we sink below the waves.

Horatio Spafford knew that feeling. He had faced more than his share of overwhelming sorrow. Like Job, he dealt with great losses in his life. He had it all and then lost it as sorrows like sea billows rolled over his life.

Horatio Gates Spafford was born on October 20, 1828, in North Troy, New York. By the time we pick up his story in the early 1870s, he had become a successful lawyer in Chicago. He was also heavily invested in Chicago's real estate along the shore of Lake Michigan. It surely appeared that he was set for life. He had a wife, Anna, and five children—four daughters and a son. Even more important, however, Spafford was a Christian. He served as a church leader; he was a friend of Dwight L. Moody (founder of Moody Bible Institute). Spafford lived his faith. George Stebbins, a gospel musician of the day, described Horatio Spafford as a "man of unusual intelligence and refinement, deeply spiritual, and a devoted student of the Scriptures."

And as a student of Scripture, surely Spafford must have read the Book of Job. Many years later, he probably wondered at the parallels of his life to that ancient man of God who lost everything, but kept his faith.

The "sorrows like sea billows" began in the early 1870s. First, Spafford's only son, Horatio Jr., died of scarlet fever. After the sorrow of a child's death, he then faced the loss of real estate holdings when the great Chicago fire swept through the city in 1871. That fire ravaged the city, leaving 300 people dead and 100,000 homeless.

Yet, though "Satan had buffeted and trials had come," Spafford had the "blest assurance" of his salvation and his faith to help him move on. For the next two years, Spafford tried to help the people of Chicago get back on their feet. He and his friend, Dwight Moody, helped the homeless, grief-stricken, and ruined people of the city to rebuild their lives—physically, emotionally, and spiritually.

After two years of sifting through the ashes and rubble of the city and of lives, Spafford decided it was time for a break for himself and his family. Dwight Moody and Ira Sankey were planning evangelistic crusades in Great Britain in 1873, so Spafford decided to help with the crusade and then continue on to Europe with his family for a vacation. Spafford booked his family on the French steamship, the *Ville de Havre*, at first choosing quarters amidships and then changing the reservation to a room closer to the bow. It appeared that everything was set for a lovely European family vacation.

At the last minute, however, business concerns in Chicago delayed Horatio's departure. He sent his wife and four daughters on ahead, promising to come a few days later and join them. It would be the last time he would see his daughters.

On November 22, 1873, off the coast of Newfoundland, the *Ville de Havre* collided with a British ship, the *Lochearn*. The *Ville de*

Havre was struck amidships and sank in only twelve minutes. Of the hundreds on board, only forty-seven survived. Spafford's four daughters—Maggie, Tanetta, Annie, and Bessie—all drowned. Miraculously, his wife Anna managed to hold onto a piece of wreckage and was rescued. (Had they remained in the original reserved room—in the amidships section—she, too, would have died.)

The survivors were taken to Wales. From there, Anna sent a telegram of just two words to her husband: "Saved alone."

With all of his children now gone and a heartbroken wife on the other side of the Atlantic, Spafford faced the billows of sorrow. He hurried to New York and sailed on the next available ship. As he crossed the Atlantic, surely he spent many hours gazing out at the sea billows rolling past. As the ship neared the waters off Newfoundland, the captain called Spafford to the bridge. He pointed to his charts and then out at the billowing waves, gently explaining that according to his calculations, the *Ville de Havre* had sunk nearby.

Gazing out at the waves that had taken his dear daughters, Spafford surely wondered why. As he cried and prayed, God brought peace to his heart. Like Job, he would never have the answer, but he had God. By the time he arrived in England, he could say to his friend, Dwight Moody, "It is well. The will of God be done."

It is well with my soul.
It is well, it is well with my soul.

In those moments on the ship when God touched his soul, the words came to Spafford. The words would one day become a hymn that would comfort millions who must face the rolling sea billows of sorrow. The words poignantly reveal—from one who himself faced great sorrow—that even in the midst of pain, it can be well with one's soul. Why? Because of what Jesus has done.

My sin—O the bliss of this glorious thought,
My sin, not in part, but the whole,
Is nailed to the cross, and I bear it no more:
Praise the Lord, praise the Lord, O my soul!

God spoke words of comfort to Horatio Spafford on the deck of that ship, and Spafford understood. In the end, all that matters is Jesus and a person's relationship with Him. Sorrow may come, but it is well with my soul. Suffering may cause me great pain, but it is well with my soul because my sin has been "nailed to the cross, and I bear it no more."

Suffering is in the world because of sin. Sin separates us from the holiness of God. Jesus took all sin upon Himself when He was nailed to the cross. When Jesus did that for us, He took the burden of sin from our shoulders. We still live in a world full of suffering and sin, but because of Jesus, it can be well with our souls.

Not only did God speak words of comfort, but also words of promise. This life is not the end, for Spafford knew that his son and daughters were safely in Jesus' arms, merely awaiting their parents' arrival one day.

And, Lord, haste the day when my faith shall be sight,
The clouds be rolled back as a scroll:
The trump shall resound and the Lord shall descend,
"Even so"—it is well with my soul.

As Spafford contemplated the return of Jesus, he may have quoted the triumphant words, "even so," from Revelation 22:20: "He who testifies to these things says, 'Surely I am coming quickly.' Amen. Even so, come, Lord Jesus!"

Come, Lord Jesus. It is well with my soul.

Our soul waits for the LORD; He is our help and our shield. For our heart shall rejoice in Him, because we have trusted in His holy name. Let Your mercy, O LORD, be upon us, just as we hope in You. PSALM 33:20–22

"Peace I leave with you, My peace I give to you; not as the world gives do I give to you. Let not your heart be troubled, neither let it be afraid." . . . "These things I have spoken to you, that in Me you may have peace. In the world you will have tribulation; but be of good cheer, I have overcome the world." JOHN 14:27; 16:33

My brethren, count it all joy when you fall into various trials, knowing that the testing of your faith produces patience. But let patience have its perfect work, that you may be perfect and complete, lacking nothing. If any of you lacks wisdom, let him ask of God, who gives to all liberally and without reproach, and it will be given to him. But let him ask in faith, with no doubting, for he who doubts is like a wave of the sea driven and tossed by the wind. JAMES 1:2–6

When sorrows like sea billows roll,

Whatever my lot,

Thou hast taught me to say,

is well with my soul.

Dear Lord,

Thank You for the promise of Your peace even in the middle of the tribulation and suffering I must face in this world. When I face difficulty, I wonder why. Help me to remember that You are with me, that You guide me, that You understand, and that You are good. Let me never forget that what really matters is my relationship with You. I ask that You will help me to say, even during trial and difficulty, that it is well with my soul. Then let me take such comfort in that knowledge that I can continue to do Your work in the world until You come to take me home.

Amen.

REFLECTIONS

from Thomas Kinkade

God's genius is seen in the details. But in the massive, unmatchable structures of creation, He reveals His awesome power and glory. By the simple measure of scale, God gives us deeper insights into the diversity of His character. It's what inspired me as I painted *The End of a Perfect Day III*, where scale enabled me to convey some key concepts. One, I wanted to illustrate the vastness of God as seen in the magnitude of the mountain behind the cottage; another, life's everyday harmony and tranquility juxtaposed against the mountain's huge frame. As the mass towers high and strong above the house, it not only emphasizes man's smallness, but it also gives a sense of comfort as an ultimate shelter and protector. To me, the comparison is a natural example of our own relationship with God, who is great enough to be feared, but also powerful enough to protect and comfort. No man-made construction can communicate such complex truth.

I was recently in Yosemite Valley and had the opportunity to watch mountain climbers scaling the sheer granite cliffs of one of the mountains. With binoculars I could see their form, their effort, and the difficulty of their task. But from a distance, they were mere pinpoints of color flanked against a wall of rock. I couldn't help but think of my life as a similar fleck of paint in the eternal scheme of things.

GOD'S SCOPE OF GREATNESS

But the scale reminded me of another aspect of God's grandeur. While the vastness drives us to Him, intimacy comes in the daily refuge of His presence. In the stillness, God meets man as his Savior and friend. He becomes both protector and confidant, shelter from without and source of comfort from within. He is great, but He meets us where we are and envelops frail, otherwise insignificant lives, and makes our purpose into mountains of greatness.

Psalm 46:1 describes God as "a refuge and strength, a very present help in trouble." Inspired by this word picture, Martin Luther penned the words to this hymn, describing God as a "mighty fortress." How many Christians across the centuries have found great comfort in the picture of God as a refuge, a place of safety to which we can run when we need protection in times of trouble. When life gets to be too much, we can run into the fortress and pull the strong gate closed behind us. There God ministers to us, protects us, and reminds us of the power we have in our Savior, Jesus Christ. Our "ancient foe," Satan, has great power and seeks to cause us trouble, but our strength is found in Christ. When we are ready, we can open the gate of the fortress and step out to continue to do battle for God in this world—covered in His armor and knowing that Christ goes with us.

A mighty fortress is our God, a bulwark never failing;
Our helper He, amid the flood of mortal ills prevailing.
For still our ancient foe doth seek to work us woe;
His craft and pow'r are great, and, armed with cruel hate,
On earth is not His equal.

This powerful hymn, one of many written by Martin Luther, has been a rallying point for believers and has stood tall among the favored hymns of the Christian church for the past five centuries.

Born on November 10, 1483, in Germany, Martin Luther was brought up in the strict atmosphere of the Roman Catholic church of the time. He was very well educated. For all of his learning, however, he was terrified by thoughts of the wrath of God. As a young man, he was constantly searching to find inward peace. After completing a master's degree, he entered an Augustinian monastery to become a monk.

In the meantime, the climate of the Catholic church at the time was increasingly political and unhealthy. For Luther, the specific problem was the sale of indulgences. A person could buy an indulgence from the church that would assure him or her the remission of sins and a shortened stay in purgatory. Luther found this to be contrary to Scripture. In 1517, special indulgences were being sold near Wittenberg. Luther used this opportunity to point out the error of this practice.

On October 31, 1517, Luther nailed his famous *Ninety-Five Theses* to the door of the cathedral in Wittenburg. These ninety-five points outlined some truths he had discovered in his personal study of God's Word. Luther did not mean his theses to be an attack on the Catholic church at large, nor did he plan for them to be known outside of Wittenberg. But even though news traveled slowly in the sixteenth century, the event was known all over Germany within two weeks.

In 1521, in the German town of Worms, Luther was asked whether he acknowledged his writings and public statements. He would retract nothing unless it could be proven to him from Scripture that he was wrong. He ended his statement to them by saying, "Here I am—God help me!" By the time Luther left Worms, he had been labeled as a heretic by Pope Leo X in the Edict of Worms.

Luther was forced into hiding for a year in Wartburg Castle. While there, he translated the Bible into German. The New Testament was printed in 1522, bringing the Word of God to the people in their daily language.

From his reading, Luther understood justification by faith and the necessity of individual faith for salvation. As his translation of

the Bible allowed the common people to read the Bible for themselves, so Luther wanted worship services to speak to the common people. He thought the best way to involve people in worship would be through singing. So he began to compose hymns and chorales that could be incorporated into worship services and sung by everyone. Between 1524 and 1545, Luther composed and compiled nine hymnals with songs that could be used in worship.

Luther's hymn, "A Mighty Fortress Is Our God" appeared in one of these hymnals. The song describes the power believers have in this world because their God is indeed a mighty fortress. The four stanzas of the hymn need to be sung one after the other, for each continues the thought from the one before. After the first stanza previously quoted that describes the power of God and the reality of our "ancient foe," the hymn continues:

Did we in our own strength confide,
Our striving would be losing;
Were not the right Man on our side,
The Man of God's own choosing.
Dost ask who that may be? Christ Jesus, it is He;
Lord Sabaoth His name, from age to age the same,
And He must win the battle.

And tho' this world, with devils filled,
Should threaten to undo us,
We will not fear, for God hath willed
His truth to triumph through us.

The prince of darkness grim—
We tremble not for him;
His rage we can endure, for lo! his doom is sure,
One little word shall fell him.

That word above all earthly pow'rs—
No thanks to them—abideth;
The Spirit and the gifts are ours
Through Him who with us sideth.
Let goods and kindred go, this mortal life also;
The body they may kill: God's truth abideth still,
His kingdom is forever.

Satan is indeed a powerful and cruel adversary of believers, but our God is more powerful still. If we trust in our own strength to fight Satan, we will lose, for we are not strong enough. But with Jesus Christ on our side, we will win the battle.

The world at times threatens to "undo us." However, we need not fear because God has planned for "His truth to triumph." And how does it triumph? "Through us." God works through His people to bring the light of His truth to this dark world. Because of God's promise, we don't need to tremble in fear of Satan, for one little word will destroy him.

That word stands strong above all powers on earth and abides, not because of them but in spite of them. As God's people, we have His Holy Spirit and the spiritual gifts that empower us to serve. As God's people, we trust in the promises of an eternal future with Him. We can let go of possessions, family, and life itself, because they are temporary. God's truth and kingdom are forever.

Yours, O LORD, is the greatness, the power and the glory, the victory and the majesty; for all that is in heaven and in earth is Yours; Yours is the kingdom, O LORD, and You are exalted as head over all. Both riches and honor come from You, and You reign over all. In Your hand is power and might; in Your hand it is to make great and to give strength to all.

1 CHRONICLES 29:11, 12

Bow down Your ear to me, deliver me speedily; be my rock of refuge, a fortress of defense to save me. For You are my rock and my fortress; therefore, for Your name's sake, lead me and guide me. PSALM 31:2, 3

Thus God, determining to show more abundantly to the heirs of promise the immutability of His counsel, confirmed it by an oath, that by two immutable things, in which it is impossible for God to lie, we might have strong consolation, who have fled for refuge to lay hold of the hope set before us. This hope we have as an anchor of the soul, both sure and steadfast.

HEBREWS 6:17–19

A mighty fortress is our God, a bulwark never failing.

Almighty God,

I praise You for being my fortress, my unfailing bulwark, my helper. I know that I am weak, but I know that You are strong. You go before me, behind me, beside me as the only One with the power to overcome Satan. I pray that You will help me to trust You always, to run to Your fortress for strength for daily living. I pray that Your truth will triumph—through me!

Amen.

Sweet Hour of Prayer

In seasons of distress and grief,
My soul has often found relief,
And oft escaped the tempter's snare
By thy return, sweet hour of prayer.

William W. Walford
1772-1850

REFLECTIONS

from Thomas Kinkade

We may not be in Eden anymore, but neither has God left us in a dark and dreary place. Despite our sin, He has seen fit to continue the blessing through the extravagant splendor of His beautiful creation. God in His grace has given us eyes that not only see shapes, but also perceive a myriad of colors that impress our moods, thoughts, and hearts. Through creation, His love for us takes visual form, enveloping those who experience it fully with the peace and harmony found in God's presence. The fact that God gave us our senses further shows His determination to lavish on us the delights of life—if we are willing to take the time to receive them.

God is eager to meet with us. Through the serenity of nature or in the midst of a busy workday, God always walks closely beside His children. He cherishes every moment we turn to Him through prayer for strength, guidance, or simply to talk. As the apostle Paul says, prayer is an activity that never ceases. Beyond words or even conscious thought, it is a state of constant communion with our Creator that allows

GOD'S GLORIOUS EMBRACE

Him into every moment of our day. Much as a child reaches up to a parent to be lifted up off the floor, our prayers place us instantly into the loving embrace of our heavenly Father. In the safety of His arms, He encourages, comforts, and teaches us His truth and equips us to participate in His plan of redemption. What an incredible blessing! Whether we're pursuing a project deadline on the job or enjoying a picnic with our family, every act in life, brought under submission to God through prayer, becomes a profound event that works to change the face of eternity.

Think about your dearest friends. The people you call when you have some great news; the ones you call when you need to share a burden that rests heavy on your heart. What a blessing those friends are. They are ready with a listening ear, rejoicing when you rejoice and weeping when you weep. They are there for you. And when they have a need, you are there for them, ready to offer the same kind of loving attention.

We may have best friends with whom to share life's joys and sorrows, but we also have another Best Friend. For believers, the God of heaven has come to earth and lives within. Before Jesus died, He told His followers, "No longer do I call you servants, for a servant does not know what his master is doing; but I have called you friends, for all things that I heard from My Father I have made known to you" (John 15:15). Imagine that! We are friends with Jesus Himself.

Now consider what it would be like if you never talked to your friends. Suppose you simply ignored those dear people in your life. What if they called and you constantly said you were too busy? What if they stopped by to see you and you hurried them out the door? What if they patiently listened to you, but when *they* needed to talk, you had no time for them? The friendship would not last long. Not only that, but you would have lost something very precious, for dear and lasting friends can be hard to find.

Communication is key in any friendship. It is no different in our friendship with Jesus. We are missing something very precious if we claim a relationship with Jesus but are constantly too busy for Him—if we attempt to hurry Him in and out of our lives, or if we simply throw our requests at Him but are too busy to hear His responses. The truth is, God wants us to sit down quietly, to talk and to listen. We are His friends, and He wants to talk with us as friends should.

Prayer is our way of communicating with our Best Friend. When we have a "sweet hour of prayer," we are indeed called away from our "world of care" and ushered right into our Friend's throne room (oh yes, our Friend is also a King!). In that throne room, we can make all our "wants and wishes known." Making them known doesn't necessarily mean that they will happen—just as when we share our desires and dreams with our friends, we know that they may not all come true. But the point is, we share. We talk. We tell our deepest needs and desires to the One who holds all of creation in His hand. We know that He has the power to meet our needs and to make our dreams reality. But we also know that He has our very best in mind and will say no if needed.

Beyond our wants and wishes, however, prayer is also a solace— a place of quiet and peace—in "seasons of distress and grief." During the times when our hearts are heavy, we go to our Friend who understands and desires to give us sweet "relief" as only He can give. When we face temptation's "snare" and are weak, our times of communication with our Friend can give us the strength to stand true. We would not want to disappoint our Friend, after all.

> *Sweet hour of prayer, sweet hour of prayer,*
> *That calls me from a world of care,*
> *And bids me at my Father's throne*
> *Make all my wants and wishes known!*
> *In seasons of distress and grief*
> *My soul has often found relief,*
> *And oft escaped the tempter's snare*
> *By thy return, sweet hour of prayer.*

Sweet hour of prayer, sweet hour of prayer,
Thy wings shall my petition bear
To Him whose truth and faithfulness
Engage the waiting soul to bless;
And since He bids me seek His face,
Believe His Word and trust His grace,
I'll cast on Him my every care,
And wait for thee, sweet hour of prayer.

Our Friend bids us to seek His face. He is never too busy, too tired, too far away. He is a breath away. His "truth and faithfulness" are waiting to bless us with His very presence. He wants us to believe His Word and trust His grace on our behalf. Because He is a perfect, good, and loving Friend, we can indeed cast our every care on Him. He is there for us—every moment of every day. Why would we not sit down for a few moments in unhurried conversation with our Best Friend?

This hymn is thought to have been written by William W. Walford in 1842. There have been a couple of stories told about this hymn. One says that he lived in the village of Coleshill, Warwickshire, England, where he both served as a lay preacher as well as the owner of a trinket shop. This first version also says that William Walford was blind. The words to this hymn about the joys of prayer had come to his mind. When his friend, Thomas Salmon, the clergyman for the area, stopped into the shop for a visit, William asked him to write down the verses as he said them.

Another version of the story is that the author was Rev. William Walford, a minister (not blind) who was president of Homerton Academy in England and the author of a book titled *The Manner of Prayer*. On a visit to the United States three years later, Salmon showed this poem to the editor of the *New York Observer*. He was so impressed that the poem appeared in the *Observer* on September 13, 1845. The music was later added by William Bradbury (who also composed music for "The Solid Rock," page 50, and "Just As I Am," page 56).

How blessed would be an hour a day spent in conversation with God. Yet the hymn does not require that we set our timers and try for sixty minutes. Instead, the picture is of a regular time with God, a regular time each day that we set aside for an appointment with Him—an appointment that nothing will cause us to miss. For in the moments we spend alone with God, we pour out our souls in thankfulness, love, and adoration. We cast off our burdens. We seek guidance. Then, we listen. In the moments of listening, we hear God speak to us words of comfort, assurance, guidance, and grace. He may also give some admonitions and warnings, as any good friend would. And we would do well to heed what He says.

Sweet hour of prayer, sweet hour of prayer,
May I thy consolation share,
Till from Mount Pisgah's lofty height
I view my home and take my flight;
This robe of flesh I'll drop, and rise
To seize the everlasting prize,
And shout, while passing through the air,
"Farewell, farewell, sweet hour of prayer!"

During those moments in quiet conversation with God, we are touching eternity. The final verse of this hymn takes us to Mount Pisgah, the peak where Moses climbed to look over into the Promised Land before he died (Deut. 34:1–5). Perhaps Mr. Walford was also thinking of Exodus 33:11, which tells us that "the LORD spoke to Moses face to face, as a man speaks to his friend."

We are God's friends. One day we, too, will drop "this robe of flesh" and "rise to seize the everlasting prize." One day we, too, will go to be with our Best Friend in His home. We can then say a fond farewell to our sweet hours of prayer, for when we get to heaven, we will be in the continual presence of God.

The LORD will command His lovingkindness in the daytime, and in the night His song shall be with me—a prayer to the God of my life. PSALM 42:8

But to You I have cried out, O LORD, and in the morning my prayer comes before You. PSALM 88:13

"But you, when you pray, go into your room, and when you have shut the door, pray to your Father who is in the secret place; and your Father who sees in secret will reward you openly." MATTHEW 6:6

Likewise the Spirit also helps in our weaknesses. For we do not know what we should pray for as we ought, but the Spirit Himself makes intercession for us with groanings which cannot be uttered. ROMANS 8:26

Be anxious for nothing, but in everything by prayer and supplication, with thanksgiving, let your requests be made known to God. PHILIPPIANS 4:6

Pray without ceasing. 1 THESSALONIANS 5:17

Thy wings shall my petition bear.

Dearest Friend,

Thank You for the privilege of prayer.

Thank You that You bid me to come to You with all my joys and sorrows, my worries, my cares, my needs, my desires. I praise You that I can talk with You about these things in my life—and that You care, You listen, and You answer. Help me to listen to You. Thank You for being my Very Best Friend. I look forward to the day when we can talk face to face!

Amen.

Need Thee Every Hour

I need Thee every hour, most gracious Lord

No tender voice like Thine can peace afford

I need Thee, O I need Thee; every hour

O bless me now, my Savior—I come to Thee

REFLECTIONS

from Thomas Kinkade

It wasn't a haphazard analogy. God calls us His sheep for a reason. Having spent much time in an agrarian setting as a rancher, I have observed these curiously clueless creatures and have seen some interesting parallels.

For starters, sheep seem to lack some critical faculties for survival—like common sense, for instance. Indeed, they may even be the most frail and dependent creatures God has made. If they fall down, someone else must pick them up. Without a shepherd, they inevitably get lost. On their own, they would surely die.

Most likely, we don't really see ourselves in that same situation of dependency. But despite the level of success we may think we have experienced, the reality is that we can accomplish absolutely nothing of eternal value apart from Him. Only His spirit working in and through us can effect true change in our hearts and reach others with His love.

Like sheep, we need our Shepherd. Also like sheep, God has put the desire to be led into our hearts. A rare trait in the animal kingdom, sheep long for someone to lead them and protect them. We do, too. And what a wonderful truth it is to realize that the Shepherd answers that need above and beyond any expectation. Trust is easy as we see Him demonstrate through history and the daily events of life His willingness to give up His life for our good. When doors of opportunity are closed, we can count it joy. The Good Shepherd knows a safer, better way, and we can trust Him to open the right gates that lead to life's greenest pastures. Like good shepherds should, Jesus guides, protects, nourishes, cleanses, and comforts us through all of life's travels. No matter what the future holds, we know that we are safe if we are resting securely in the Shepherd's arms.

SAFE WITH THE SHEPHERD

I need Thee every hour, most gracious Lord;
No tender voice like Thine can peace afford.
I need Thee, O I need Thee; every hour I need Thee!
O bless me now, my Savior—I come to Thee!

Time. We all have the same amount of it every day. Twenty-four hours during which to accomplish our tasks and take our rest. Yet time is not static. How often do we say, "Time is just flying by!" "I just don't have enough hours in the day." "Where has the time gone?" "It only seems like yesterday . . ."? Yes, time keeps moving and we move along with it.

With what do we fill those precious twenty-four-hour blocks of time? Perhaps it is a job that requires our presence—of body and of mind. Perhaps we are at home with young children who require massive amounts of our own limited energy in order to keep up with theirs. Maybe we're at the middle time of life when our own schedule vies for attention against the schedules of the other people in our lives who need us to be there, take them here, or watch them do that. We fill our lives and our day planners with all kinds of activity, sometimes taking pride in our busyness. Of course, most of our activities are important. But have we sought what is *most* important? In other words, have we set our priorities correctly?

This hymn wasn't written by a preacher or a missionary, nor was it born of great distress. Annie Sherwood Hawks wrote the words to this hymn when she was a thirty-seven-year-old busy homemaker and mother of three children. Born in Hoosick, New York, on May 28, 1835, she showed early in life that she was a gifted verse writer. By the time she was fourteen years old she was already contributing her poems to various newspapers for publication. In 1859, she married Charles Hawks. They lived in Brooklyn, New York, and were members of Hanson Place Baptist Church.

All in all, she had what sounds like a pretty normal life—much like the lives most of us lead. Busy, yet sometimes somewhat mundane. We go to work every day. We clean the house. We care for children. We go about our routines. We serve at school and at church. We wash the laundry and pay the bills. While most of what we do is important, sometimes we take on extraneous activities that pack our schedules and cause us stress. At those times when we have allowed ourselves to get overwhelmed by our routines, we need to cut back, say no, and set priorities.

Annie Hawks understood, as we must, that even for living our "normal" lives, we desperately need our Savior. We need Him every hour. He alone can bring peace to our hectic days or meaning to the mundane. He alone can help us to set priorities and make sure that we have the time for what is most important. He understands what it means to have much on our shoulders and seemingly little time in which to do it. He wants us to sit down quietly for a few moments and let Him tell us what *He* wants us to do. He wants us to give Him our schedules so that He can arrange our lives to complete exactly what He wants us to do—no more, no less.

I need Thee every hour, stay Thou near by;
Temptations lose their power when Thou art nigh.
I need Thee, O I need Thee; every hour I need Thee!
O bless me now, my Savior—I come to Thee!

Every day is filled with surprises. Do we awaken with joy at what God might have planned for us, or are we afraid to come out from under the covers? When we step into our daily routines, we step into a world filled with difficulties and temptations. How can we cope? By taking Jesus with us into the day. From the moment we awaken, He is there. He talks with us as we dress for the day; He

rides with us in the car; He sits with us at work or in the meeting or at the appointment; He is there during the difficult assignment or the tedious routine. When Jesus stays nearby, we are strengthened. We do indeed need Him every hour. When temptations come along, they lose their power because we are very aware of the presence of our Savior.

Annie Hawks was encouraged in her poetic writing by her pastor, Dr. Robert Lowry, who was himself a poet and musician. About this hymn she wrote that, as a young wife and mother, she was busy with her household tasks. Then, on a June morning in 1872, "Suddenly I became filled with the sense of nearness to the Master, and I began to wonder how anyone could ever live without Him, either in joy or pain. Then the words were ushered into my mind."

I need Thee every hour, in joy or pain;
Come quickly and abide, or life is vain.
I need Thee, O I need Thee; every hour I need Thee!
O bless me now, my Savior—I come to Thee!

What is life worth if we are not living for something beyond ourselves? What if these fleeting moments are all there is—no eternal future, nothing to live for, nothing to die for? We would be most miserable, for we would have to spend our lives attempting to amass as much as we could for the short time of enjoyment, only then to leave it all behind. Without Christ, life would indeed be vain.

Fortunately, our time on earth is filled with meaning—eternal meaning. We are part of a plan, like a thread in a beautiful tapestry. Without our part, something would be missing. We are not mistakes; our lives are not meaningless. We are worth so much that Christ came to die for us.

He alone gives meaning to life. We need Him every hour, for our days will be filled with times of joy and times of pain. We need Him every hour, for He alone can give us the eternal perspective that allows us to trust Him and live for Him no matter what our circumstances.

I need Thee every hour, Most Holy One;
O make me Thine indeed, Thou blessed Son!
I need Thee, O I need Thee; every hour I need Thee!
O bless me now, my Savior—I come to Thee!

Annie Hawks wrote the four stanzas to this poem and showed them to her pastor. Lowry himself then composed the music for the verses and added the refrain. The hymn appeared in a small book of hymns prepared for the National Baptist Sunday School Association Convention in Cincinnati, Ohio, in 1872. The song became very well known when D. L. Moody and Ira Sankey used it in their evangelistic campaigns in America and Great Britain.

The song has blessed many people as they consider their need for the Savior to be with them "every hour." Annie Hawks herself barely understood the power of her own words until she faced the difficult days following the death of her husband. She wrote that she did not understand why the hymn had touched so many people until the shadow of the loss of her husband fell across her life. Then she wrote, "I understood something of the comforting power in the words, which I had been permitted to give out to others in my hour of sweet serenity and peace."

What are you doing with the twenty-four hours allotted to you today? Are your priorities in order? No matter how busy your schedule, have you put Christ in charge of every hour? You need Him every hour. When He is Lord of your hours, your life becomes filled with meaning, with peace, with joy, and with the knowledge that you are doing exactly what you need to do—for you are doing His will.

I need Thee, O I need Thee; every hour I need Thee!
O bless me now, my Savior—I come to Thee!

The LORD shall preserve your going out and your coming in from this time forth, and even forevermore. PSALM 121:8

To everything there is a season, a time for every purpose under heaven. ECCLESIASTES 3:1

Now it is high time to awake out of sleep; for now our salvation is nearer than when we first believed. The night is far spent, the day is at hand. Therefore let us cast off the works of darkness, and let us put on the armor of light. Let us walk properly. . . . Put on the Lord Jesus Christ, and make no provision for the flesh, to fulfill its lusts. ROMANS 13:11–14

See then that you walk circumspectly, not as fools but as wise, redeeming the time, because the days are evil. Therefore do not be unwise, but understand what the will of the Lord is.

EPHESIANS 5:15–17

Most Gracious Lord,

I do need You every hour. I need to know Your presence with me every moment of every day. I ask for Your guidance as I go into my day today. Help me to set priorities, to know when to say no, to be able to accomplish the tasks at hand. Give me wisdom so that I might well use the gifts You have given me.

I come to You today. Bless me now, my Savior. Amen.

O for a Thousand Tongues to Sing

Jesus! the name that charms our fears,
That bids our sorrows cease;
'Tis music in the sinner's ears,
'Tis life and health and peace.

Charles Wesley
1707-1788

REFLECTIONS

from Thomas Kinkade

So you've blown it. Again. Just when you think you've gotten on top of things, you find yourself under that same old stubborn pile of sin that stops you dead in your tracks. Where do you go now? What hope is left?

Praise be to God for His indescribable gift! With our incredible Savior's promise of forgiveness, there is not enough sin to pile on one day that the next there wouldn't be His open arms welcoming us back. Like the dawning of a new day, our souls are wiped clean under the cleansing power of His blood whenever we come to Him confessing our sins. And why not come? Our Creator knows us. He sees our frailties. He knows our propensity to go astray. But Christ is the God of new beginnings, and His mercies are new every morning.

The good news doesn't stop there. The cleansing that Jesus brings goes beyond the symptoms of our sin. It penetrates to our hearts where roots of wrongdoing begin. His love heals the wounds that past pain from others have caused. It enables us to forgive, as well. And then His love begins the transformation in our hearts—the kind that turns our tendency toward rebellion into a tender submission to His spirit. We are made whole. New. And the song of forgiveness and freedom rings ever so sweetly in our ears.

NEW BEGINNINGS

O for a thousand tongues to sing
My great Redeemer's praise,
The glories of my God and King,
The triumphs of His grace!

Sometimes we forget to be thankful. When we get wrapped up in the worries and cares of our daily lives, we often are overwhelmed by the troubles that come our way. Our perspective would be completely changed if we took the energy we put into worry and funneled it into praise. When we find ourselves in the midst of care and worry, we could sing our great Redeemer's praise—raising our voices to His glory and to the triumphs that His amazing grace has brought into our lives. In one of his many psalms, David wrote: "My tongue shall speak of Your righteousness and of Your praise all the day long" (Ps. 35:28). Clearly, there is a place for praise in the daily life of every believer.

David wrote many songs that call to us from the pages of our Bibles. Like him, Charles Wesley was also a prolific songwriter. It has been argued that he is probably one of the most influential hymn writers ever, for he wrote 6,500 hymn texts. He was constantly writing poetry, finding expression for people's most heartfelt desires and needs in the words that came to him as he rode on horseback and preached throughout England.

Charles Wesley is perhaps less well known than his older brother, the fiery preacher named John Wesley. Charles was born on December 18, 1707, the eighteenth of nineteen children. Their father, Samuel Wesley, wanted his sons to be educated and to become clergymen. Charles went to Oxford University.

While there, Charles struggled with spiritual matters. In 1729, he and some friends, also concerned about personal spirituality, began what came to be called the "Holy Club." Their methodical habits and seriousness earned them the nickname "methodists." Because Charles had started the club, he can be called the first Methodist. Charles' brother John later became leader of the group. It seems that both men were seeking a way to answer the deep spiritual questions in their lives.

My gracious Master and my God,
Assist me to proclaim,
To spread through all the earth abroad
The honors of Thy name.

At the end of 1735, Charles went with his brother John to America as missionaries to the colony of Georgia. The time there, however, proved to be unsuccessful. They had great difficulty and returned, disillusioned, to England—Charles first, then John the next year. Charles hoped to be able to return to Georgia someday, but a severe illness changed those plans.

However, on the voyage to America, the brothers had met a group of German believers on the ship. These believers were Moravians, and their spiritual depth and songs of praise impressed the Wesleys. After their trip to America and return to England, both men again came into contact with Moravian believers. It was with them, at a meeting in Aldersgate, London, in May 1738 that both brothers realized that they had never personally accepted Jesus Christ as personal Savior. When they both accepted Christ, their ministries took on new power.

Jesus! the name that charms our fears,
That bids our sorrows cease;
'Tis music in the sinner's ears,
'Tis life and health and peace.

Both Charles and John Wesley were known for their preaching and teaching—traveling thousands of miles on horseback throughout Great Britain conducting public services, often for thousands of people at a time. Charles was a beloved preacher, but was also many times persecuted for his straightforward presentation of the gospel message and the need for that message to make a difference in people's lives. His evangelist friend, George Whitefield, decried the many preachers who spoke from the pulpit of a Christ they didn't seem to know or feel. The genuineness and passion of men like the Wesleys and Whitefield caused many to rediscover a faith that mattered.

Does your faith make a difference in your daily life? Is it dead with boring routine or alive with power? Do you sense the joy behind your faith, joy that could be filled with the praise of "a thousand tongues"? Is the name of Jesus "music to your ears"? Faith is meant to make a difference in our lives, today and every day. Genuine faith makes you want to sing in praise to God. Life with Christ is not meant to be drudgery; it is to be "life and health and peace."

Jesus brings *true life*. "I have come that they may have life, and that they may have it more abundantly" (John 10:10).

Jesus brings *true health*. "The Spirit of the LORD is upon Me. . . . He has sent Me to heal the brokenhearted" (Luke 4:18).

Jesus brings *true peace*. "Peace I leave with you, My peace I give to you; not as the world gives do I give to you. Let not your heart be troubled, neither let it be afraid" (John 14:27).

He breaks the power of canceled sin,
He sets the prisoner free;
His blood can make the foulest clean,
His blood availed for me.

So we praise Him. We may have only one tongue, but with it we should praise Him who has broken the power of sin in our lives and set us free from its prison. We can praise Him for shedding His blood so that our sin could be washed away.

Hear Him, ye deaf; His praise, ye dumb,
Your loosened tongues employ;
Ye blind, behold your Savior come;
And leap, ye lame, for joy!

No matter what we face today, the future is sure with Christ. No matter what difficulties block our way today, one day, Christ will make all things right. The deaf will hear, the mute will sing, the blind will see, the lame will leap for joy. The difficulties of today will be transformed into the joy of tomorrow.

This hymn was written in 1749, and it is said that it was meant to celebrate the eleventh anniversary of Charles Wesley's conversion. The words may have come from the Moravian leader, Peter Bohler, who had said at one time, "Had I a thousand tongues, I would praise Christ Jesus with all of them."

Believers can take this song of praise and use it to remember what Christ has done for them. All honor, glory, and praise go to Him who made us and then brought us to Himself. There is much to be thankful for today. Praise the Lord!

O for a thousand tongues to sing
My great Redeemer's praise,
The glories of my God and King,
The triumphs of His grace!

You shall fear the LORD your God; you shall serve Him, and to Him you shall hold fast, and take oaths in His name. He is your praise, and He is your God, who has done for you these great and awesome things which your eyes have seen.
DEUTERONOMY 10:20, 21

I will praise You, O LORD, with my whole heart;
I will tell of all Your marvelous works.
I will be glad and rejoice in You;
I will sing praise to Your name, O Most High. PSALM 9:1, 2

Sing praise to the LORD, You saints of His,
and give thanks at the remembrance of His holy name.
PSALM 30:4

Therefore by Him let us continually offer the sacrifice of praise to God, that is, the fruit of our lips, giving thanks to His name. HEBREWS 13:15

The glories of my God and King,
The triumphs of His grace.

My Great Redeemer,

I desire to praise You for all that You have done for me. You have charmed my fears and bid my sorrows to cease. You have brought me life and health and peace. You broke the power of sin in my life and set me free. You have made me clean before You. Glory and praise to You forever! I praise You today and every day.

Thank You for what You have done for me.

Amen.

The Solid Rock

The Solid Rock

Edward Mote, 1797-1874

1. My   hope is built
2. When dark-ness veils
3. His   oath, His cov-
4. When   He shall come

When He shall come with trumpet sound,

O may I then in Him be found,

Dressed in His righteous

Faultless to stand before the throne

Edward Mote
1797-1874

REFLECTIONS
from Thomas Kinkade

I encountered the concept through a gospel song. For years I struggled with the thought, contemplating how to capture it on canvas. Then through the last part of a seven-year series I saw the light. God is our Rock of Salvation—and what better way to convey the hope and guidance He radiates than through a rugged lighthouse, situated atop the solid, unmoving mass of rocks as the tumultuous waves of the sea crash against it.

For the ships that near the harbor, whether in a storm or simply the darkness of a passing day, the lighthouse beacon becomes an anchor of safety. Follow its faithful beam and bypass all the hazards of hidden rocks, unknown obstacles, and shallow waters. It's a graphic depiction of the gospel's hope: the powerful, immutable, and radiant Christ who becomes our bulwark against the rocky seas, our guide past life's unseen dangers, and our light that leads us safely home.

But the beacon of hope is not for us alone. It is meant to be shared. As many as will heed the Savior's call will share in the benefits and blessings His shelter provides. Our hope is built on nothing less, and neither is theirs. They must see. They most know. And we must help them find the way to the Light that will bring them life, too.

LIGHT THE WAY

On what is your hope built? Do you have high hopes for your children, your marriage, your new job, your new location? Unless we're hopeless pessimists, we generally have hopes for life to go well or even to improve. But when we talk about "hope," we're referring to something that we'd like to happen but we know very well may not. We hope, leaving the door open for disappointment.

When believers talk about salvation and heaven, however, we use the word "hope," but we speak in the Bible's terminology. The Bible says, "For we were saved in this hope, but hope that is seen is not hope; for why does one still hope for what he sees? But if we hope for what we do not see, we eagerly wait for it with perseverance" (Rom. 8:24, 25). When the Bible talks about "hope," it has a totally different perspective. The "hope" of salvation and eternal life never leaves the door open for disappointment.

How can we be so sure of something in which we "hope"? Because our "hope is built on nothing less than Jesus' blood and righteousness." We do not hope in a fairy tale, we do not hope in a reward that may or may not come depending on how good we have been, and we do not hope based on anything we do or do not do in this life. Our hope is based on the fact that the righteous, sinless Jesus shed His blood on the cross for our sins. *He died for us.* Someone who died for us is not going to then allow us to slip away on a technicality! He paid the ultimate price to assure our salvation. And because God "did not spare His own Son, but delivered Him up for us all, how shall He not with Him also freely give us all things?" (Rom. 8:32).

Our hope is built on Jesus Christ, the solid Rock of our salvation. To build our hope on anything else—our family's faith,

My hope is built on nothing less
Than Jesus' blood and righteousness;
I dare not trust the sweetest frame,
But wholly lean on Jesus' name.
On Christ, the solid Rock, I stand—
All other ground is sinking sand,
All other ground is sinking sand.

our personal goodness, our generosity, our national heritage—is to be standing on nothing more solid than quicksand.

This hymn was written in 1834 by Edward Mote, a native of London, England. Born on January 21, 1797, Mote grew up in the streets of London—his parents managed a pub, often leaving young Edward to manage himself. He did not have the privilege of a godly upbringing; indeed, he once wrote, "So ignorant was I that I did not know that there was a God."

But God sought out young Edward. When he was a young man, Mote began a cabinetmaking apprenticeship and became very skilled in the trade. Even as Mote learned to fashion cabinets, God was working to fashion his life. When he was still a teenager, Mote was taken by the master craftsman from whom he was learning to hear pastor John Hyatt. At that time, Mote was converted to Christ. He truly had nothing on which to stand for his acceptance by Christ, but he understood the good news of Christ's sacrifice for him.

The same is true for all people. We have nothing to bring to Christ except our broken and sinful lives. We have nothing that we can use to claim to make ourselves acceptable to Him. The only thing we can claim is Christ's blood and righteousness.

So we come. Bringing our emptiness for Christ to fill. And fill us He does. He walks into our dirty lives and makes them clean. He walks into our pain and hurt and brings comfort and healing. And He takes up residence in us, ready to walk with us through the remaining days of our lives.

Does Christ then make it all easy and carefree? Is life with Christ an allegorical "walk in the park"? No, for Jesus Himself told us, "In the world you will have tribulation" (John 16:33). Sometimes the

"hope" is all we have to hold onto during times of great difficulty.

Sometimes darkness seems to veil the face of Christ. Sometimes darkness comes into our lives like a thick fog and feels as though it will suffocate us. Have we ceased to be believers? Have we lost our faith? Have we lost Christ?

No. We are simply being human. We are simply facing overwhelming feelings. What we must do during those times is simply hold on. Christ does not move, He does not change, and so we "rest on His unchanging grace." Our salvation is sure because He is the solid Rock; in times of difficulty, however, we must hold on to His unchanging grace. We must throw out our anchor and keep our ship close to port, so that the high winds and stormy gale cannot send us floundering out on a sea of doubt and despair. And as the rains come down and the flood threatens to sink us, when even our soul itself seems to give way, we know that His oath and covenant (His promises to us) and His shed blood on the cross are our sure support. He promises to keep us, to hold us, to help us. Yes, in the world we will have tribulation, but Jesus also added, "Be of good cheer, I have overcome the world" (John 16:33).

Edward Mote had become a Christian and he continued to be a successful cabinetmaker, surely thankful to his master craftsman for introducing him to *the* Master Craftsman. He continued in this career for over thirty years. Apparently as he sawed and fashioned his cabinets, his mind often went to his faith. He describes the writing of this hymn as occurring as he was working. He wanted to write a hymn about "the gracious experience of a Christian." The chorus came first, and then during the day, four verses came to

When darkness seems to hide his face,
I rest on His unchanging grace;
In every high and stormy gale
My anchor holds within the veil.

His oath, His covenant, His blood
Support me in the whelming flood;
When all around my soul gives way,
He then is all my hope and stay.

mind (his original hymn had six verses). He wrote them down and put them in his pocket.

The following Sunday, a friend asked him to come and visit his wife who was at home very ill. They were going to sing a hymn together, but his friend could not find his hymnbook. Mote mentioned that he had some verses he had written in his pocket, and so he pulled them out and sang them to the ill woman. She enjoyed them so much, that Mote copied them down for her to keep. That evening, two more verses were penned and taken to her. The effect of the words of this hymn on the dying woman was so profound that Mote knew this was something special, so he had them printed for distribution.

Edward Mote wrote more than one hundred texts for hymns during his lifetime. His *Hymns of Praise* was published in 1836. This hymn was included under the title, "The Immutable Basis of a Sinner's Hope."

At age fifty, Mote became pastor of a Baptist church in Horsham, Sussex, for the next twenty-six years. Through his tireless efforts, a building for his congregation was built. So beloved was he by the congregation and so grateful were they to him for the building that they offered him the deed to the property. He refused it, saying, "I do not want the chapel; I only want the pulpit, and when I cease to preach Christ, then turn me out of that." Apparently, he never stopped preaching Christ, for he continued in the pulpit until ill health forced him to resign in 1873 at age seventy-six. He died the following year. On his tombstone were inscribed the following words: "In loving memory of Mr. Edward Mote, who fell asleep in Jesus November 13th, 1874, aged 77 years. For 26 years the beloved pastor of this church, preaching Christ and Him crucified, as all the sinner can need, and all the saint desire."

When He shall come with trumpet sound,
O may I then in Him be found;
Dressed in His righteousness alone,
Faultless to stand before the throne.

When we die, we will all stand before God's throne. What will we say to Christ then? We cannot say that we tried to be good, or that we thought we were doing right, or that we had a good family. All that will matter at that moment will be whether we are standing on Christ, the solid Rock, dressed in His righteousness and, therefore, faultless before Him.

On Christ, the solid Rock, I stand—
All other ground is sinking sand,
All other ground is sinking sand.

He is the Rock, His work is perfect; for all His ways are justice, a God of truth and without injustice; righteous and upright is He. DEUTERONOMY 32:4

The LORD is my rock and my fortress and my deliverer. . . . For who is God, except the LORD? And who is a rock, except our God? . . . The LORD lives! Blessed be my Rock! Let God be exalted, the Rock of my salvation! 2 SAMUEL 22:2, 32, 47

Let us hold fast the confession of our hope without wavering, for He who promised is faithful. HEBREWS 10:23

My Savior, my Rock,

Thank You that I am saved by Your blood and righteousness alone. Thank You that even during times of darkness and difficulty, I can rest on Your unchanging grace. Thank You for being the solid Rock on which all my hopes can stand secure. And thank You for the privilege of knowing with certainty that one day I will stand before You dressed in the robes of Your righteousness, faultless because of Your sacrifice for me. Amen.

Christ, the solid Rock, I stand

Just As I Am

Just as I am, without one plea,

But that Thy blood was shed for me,

And that Thou bidd'st me come to Thee,

O Lamb of God, I come! I come!

Charlotte Elliot
1789-1871

REFLECTIONS

from Thomas Kinkade

Religion, I have heard said, is man's attempt to reach God. Whether through good works, rules, restrictions, or withdrawal from life, we innately feel the need to earn a position of favor through our behavior before God's throne (or at least to have something to say for ourselves). But Jesus doesn't call us to religion. He desires a relationship with us. One with no strings attached. One where all the debts are paid, all expectations met, and only love and support exist. It's a relationship like no other.

He is able to welcome us sinners, just as we are, for one simple reason: He bought us. He paid for our souls with His own holy blood. Exchanging His righteousness for our filthy rags of sin, He covers us with the perfection God requires in all of His children. And we don't have to do anything to get this gift except receive it. It doesn't sound fair—it's certainly nothing we deserve—but it's all a part of God's incredible plan of forgiveness.

Whenever I begin to forget this blessed truth and buy instead into Satan's lie that I must earn

NO STRINGS ATTACHED

God's love, I follow this exercise: I ask myself, *How many of my sins were in the future when Christ died for them?* Answer: all of them. *Does that mean that your sins are forgiven?* Yes. In fact, the Bible says that "while we were still sinners, Christ died for us" (Rom. 5:8). He didn't wait until we could get our act together before He wanted us. He wants us just as we are. And as we learn to rest in the beautiful work He has done in our hearts, our lives also begin to change. We turn away from our sin because our desire is to please Him, and sin's grip on our lives loses its hold. Then His love molds us into His own image, where our lives become the very reflection of His light in us.

If you were to take a poll and ask people if they like themselves "just as they are," you'd probably get a large array of answers—in the negative. Some people might not like anything about themselves; others would like to be a little richer, a little thinner, a little more outgoing, a little less outgoing, taller, shorter, more successful, more spiritual, more organized, more healthy. Maybe one in a thousand would say, "Yes, I like myself just as I am—I wouldn't change a thing!"

While there is always room for self-improvement, the inability of most people to accept themselves as they are goes to the very root of their being. Some things we can work to change or do better; other things cannot be changed, and we would do well to learn to accept ourselves as we are—to accept ourselves as God made us and as He accepts us.

Just as I am, without one plea,
But that Thy blood was shed for me,
And that Thou bidd'st me come to Thee,
O Lamb of God, I come!
I come!

The author of this hymn learned the hard way about accepting herself, for God allowed some unexpected and unpleasant changes in her life. She had known a carefree and active life, but then a disease changed everything. Watching her life change quickly from all she had known to all that she had never desired caused periods of great introspection and even anger at God. But through her difficulty came the words of this hymn (originally written as a poem) that have stirred millions to come to the Savior who accepts them just as they are.

The author of this text was Charlotte Elliott. Born in Clapham, England, on March 18, 1789, Charlotte grew up to become a popular portrait artist and writer of humorous verse. Her father was vicar of Clapham; her brother followed his father into the ministry.

Charlotte was known for her carefree ways and enjoyed life immensely. Then everything changed. In 1819, at age thirty, her health suddenly began to fail. Her body faced a serious ailment that left her with feelings of overpowering weakness and exhaustion, forcing her to spend most of each day in bed, a virtual invalid.

This would be enough to spin many of us into dark depression, and it was no different for Charlotte. She became increasingly sad and despondent. Her inability to accomplish anything at all forced her to question God's love and concern for her as well as to question her value as a human being.

Then in 1822, the light began to dawn. Her father invited a friend to dinner in their home—a prominent evangelist and minister from Switzerland named Dr. Caesar Malan. At the dinner table, the conversation turned to spiritual matters and Charlotte expressed her pain. The minister spoke to Charlotte about her need to become a Christian and give her burdens to Christ. Charlotte was offended by his comment, but it shook her to the core.

A few weeks later, she met Dr. Milan again and, by then, had sensed a burning desire in her heart. At that point, she told him that she had been trying to find the Savior, but did not know how to come to Him.

His answer? "Just come to Him as you are." He told Charlotte that she could come to the Savior with her pain, her doubts, her fears, her anger, and that Christ would put His love in their place.

From that moment, Charlotte's life was changed. She never regained her health, but she had gone from despair to faith.

Indeed, when we come to Christ, we have not "one plea"—nothing to recommend us except the blood of Christ that has been shed for us. He bids us to come to Him. He is calling.

Just as I am, and waiting not
To rid my soul of one dark blot,
To Thee whose blood can cleanse each spot,
O Lamb of God, I come! I come!

We need not wait to come to the Savior. We don't need to clean up our lives before He will accept us. The blood of Christ alone can cleanse us of sin, and so we must first come to Him, "waiting not," so that His "blood can cleanse each spot." Christ died not for saints, but for sinners. Sinners just like us. He takes us just as we are.

Just as I am, though tossed about
With many a conflict, many a doubt,
Fightings and fears within, without,
O Lamb of God, I come! I come!

Likewise, we need not resolve all of our doubts, fears, and questions before we come to the Savior. We may feel tossed about with many conflicts, many doubts, facing internal and external battles. Only Christ can help us make sense of them all. Only Christ offers the freedom and forgiveness we so desperately need. Like Charlotte, we don't need to understand the answers—we simply need to come as we are—weak, helpless, burdened, alone, sick—and let God do His mighty work in us.

Just as I am, poor, wretched, blind;
Sight, riches, healing of the mind,
Yea, all I need in Thee to find,
O Lamb of God, I come! I come!

We come as we are, "poor, wretched, blind," and we find in Christ "sight, riches, and healing." Not that Christ takes away all of our problems—He did not heal Charlotte's illness—but He gives the answers He knows we need the most. He did not heal Charlotte's body, but He healed her mind. And God used her illness to allow her to write these words that would change lives across the globe. These blessed words have allowed many people who have been unable to accept themselves to comprehend for the first time that God accepts them—just as they are.

The words of this hymn were not immediately written upon Charlotte's conversion. In fact, it wasn't until fourteen years later that Charlotte penned them. Obviously the impact of Dr. Milan's words had stayed with her for many years.

In the meantime, her brother had become vicar of the parish in Brighton. He desired to build a school for the children of poor clergymen. He began raising the funds for this endeavor. He held bazaars and other types of fund-raising projects, but Charlotte could not be of any help to him because of her illness.

There was one thing she could do, however, and that was to write poetry. She had been writing poetry for many years, and so she sat down to pen a poem that she hoped to sell to generate income for the school. The little phrase that had changed her life, "Just come to Him as you are," formed the basis for her poem, and her own experiences filled in the rest. The sale of this poem brought in more funds for her brother's school than all of his other fund-raising efforts combined! The poem was published in 1836 along with the second edition of a collection of her poetry called *The Invalid's Hymn Book.*

Just as I am, Thou wilt receive,
Wilt welcome, pardon, cleanse, relieve;
Because Thy promise I believe,
O Lamb of God, I come! I come!

And so, we come. Sinners needing grace and forgiveness. Poor, wretched, blind, afraid, alone, burdened, depressed, rebellious. We come. And just as we are, Christ receives us. He wraps us in His strong, loving arms with welcome, pardon, cleansing, and sweet relief.

Come to the Lamb of God. Believe His promise to save you. He will receive you just as you are.

"Come to Me, all you who labor and are heavy laden, and I will give you rest." MATTHEW 11:28

"The Spirit of the LORD is upon Me, because He has anointed Me to preach the gospel to the poor; He has sent Me to heal the brokenhearted, to proclaim liberty to the captives and recovery of sight to the blind, to set at liberty those who are oppressed." LUKE 4:18

"All that the Father gives Me will come to Me, and the one who comes to Me I will by no means cast out." JOHN 6:37

That you, being rooted and grounded in love, may be able to comprehend with all the saints what is the width and length and depth and height—to know the love of Christ which passes knowledge; that you may be filled with all the fullness of God. EPHESIANS 3:17–19

To Thee whose blood can cleanse each spot,

O Lamb of God, I come!

Dearest Jesus,

Thank You for accepting me just as I am.

Thank You that I can come to You assured of Your welcome, knowing that You will pardon and cleanse me and bring sweet relief to my soul. Dear Jesus, today and every day, I come.

Amen.

Battle Hymn of the Republic

In the beauty of the lilies

Christ was born across the sea,

With a glory in

that transfigures you and me,

Julia W. Howe
1819-1910

REFLECTIONS

from Thomas Kinkade

As my feet neared the edge of the ledge and my eyes caught sight of the glory before me, I stood speechless. Yosemite Valley sprawled before me, and it was the most profound, emotionally moving experience with nature that I've ever had. It was as if I had stepped before the very throne of God and seen His face in the massive outcroppings of mountains, intermingled with clouds and splashes of sun that united the two firmaments in one incredible power. Nature echoed in land and in sky the very vastness and glory of God in a way nothing else on earth could describe. My soul was caught up in praise, and I marveled at God's goodness to give me a glimpse of His awesome power.

I realize now, perhaps even more so than back then, what a solid statement of God's truth these mountains make to me. Like so many of the national parks scattered throughout our great nation, these pockets of preserved creation remind me of the sure, pure, and spiritual foundation on which our country was established. No matter what ills befall us or what enemies may try to come against us, our roots are embedded in the rock of Christ, much like the mountains remain a permanent fixture in the landscape. I am not saying that all Americans are believers. But because of our forefathers' efforts to weave biblical principles into every aspect of our nation's inception, we are still reaping the benefits and unity of those efforts. Other nations may be blessed financially as we are, but America stands apart as a nation that consistently seeks the better good of herself and others around her. We live to beat injustice. To help others. To create a better world. It is the remnant calling from God that even hardened hearts in today's culture can hardly ignore. His truth is a fire that still flames in our hearts. *Our God is marching on*.

A SURE FOUNDATION

When Jesus was being tried before the Roman governor, Pilate asked the intriguing question, "What is truth?" (John 18:38). Still today, many people ask the same question. Indeed, what is truth? Is my truth the same as your truth? Can't we have different truths?

Those who claim to love God and His Word understand, however, that there are absolute truths. People can disagree about many things, but when it comes down to many basics of life, God speaks the final truth and His truth is absolute. His truth will always be marching on, for His truth will never be overtaken—no matter what lies are placed against it.

Julia Ward Howe saw in God's Word the truth of people's equality before Him. Abraham Lincoln had become President of the United States, but the Civil War was threatening the unity of the country. Lincoln strongly condemned the institution of slavery as morally wrong and believed that black people should have the rights delineated in the Declaration of Independence—life, liberty, and the pursuit of happiness.

Hostilities between the North and the South increased. Then came the raid on Harper's Ferry that served as a culmination. A man named John Brown was an abolitionist (favored the abolishing of slavery). He had been working for years to rally an army of slaves to force the South to its knees. Some abolitionists in the North financed his raid on the federal arsenal at Harpers Ferry. On October 16, 1859, Brown and a small group of followers captured two plantation owners and recruited their slaves. The mission ended badly, however. Brown ended up tried in a Virginia court,

Mine eyes have seen the glory of the coming of the Lord,
He is trampling out the vintage where the grapes of wrath are stored;
He hath loosed the fateful lightning of His terrible swift sword,
His truth is marching on.

convicted of treason, and hanged. From the event came a call to war and a wildly popular song called "John Brown's Body."

Clearly, the North and the South were not going to come to a peaceful resolution. Julia Ward Howe would make her mark during this time of upheaval. She was born on May 27, 1819, in New York City. She later married Dr. Samuel Howe, a prominent humanitarian and abolitionist in Boston. Julia shared his vehement beliefs against slavery.

As the country heated up for war, the Howes were touring Union army camps near Washington D.C.—her husband as part of President Lincoln's Military Sanitary Commission. With them was a pastor, Rev. James Freeman Clarke. During the course of their visit, they heard the soldiers singing the popular song, "John Brown's Body." The song was serving as a call to arms and an inspiration, despite its rather notorious lyrics. The pastor, who knew that Julia had already done some published writing, suggested that she write new lyrics to the song, lyrics that would be inspiring in a much more powerful manner. She replied that the same thought had crossed her mind.

She then tells the story of awakening the next morning in the gray dawn and, to her astonishment, finding the lines arranging themselves in her head. She lay very still until they all were there, and then she jumped up quickly to write them down before they disappeared.

Clearly, she saw the coming Civil War as a battle against right and wrong—God's truth against humanity's lies. She sensed the battle as being God's very judgment against her beloved country that was allowing people within its realm to be owned and enslaved by others. The truth as she understood it from God's Word would be marching on the heels of those who fought against slavery.

I have seen Him in the watchfires
Of a hundred circling camps,
They have builded Him an altar
In the evening dews and damps;
I can read His righteous sentence
By the dim and flaring lamps,
His day is marching on.

He has sounded forth the trumpet
That shall never sound retreat,
He is sifting out the hearts of men
Before His judgment seat,
O be swift, my soul, to answer Him!
Be jubilant, my feet!
Our God is marching on.

In the visit to the Union Army camp, she saw the fires outside the tents as though they were altars and the trumpet call as a battle cry. The encouragement to join in this righteous cause comes in the words "be swift, my soul, to answer Him; be jubilant my feet!" Follow God into battle, for His truth is marching on.

The words to Julia's song first appeared for the public in the *Atlantic Monthly Magazine* in 1862, right on the cover. They were recognized immediately as a call to battle for the republic, and soon the song was being sung fervently. At one time, the song was being sung by a soloist at a rally attended by President Lincoln. At the end, the song was met with thunderous applause, and Lincoln requested that it be sung again.

In the beauty of the lilies
Christ was born across the sea,
With a glory in His bosom
That transfigures you and me;
As He died to make men holy,
Let us die to make men free,
While God is marching on.

The call to battle ends with a picture of Christ Himself, filled with a glory that changes people from within. As He died to make people holy, then we, too, should be willing to die to make them free. This call to fight against the slavery of people who should be free Americans resonated with many in the North who took up arms. They would fight a battle and refuse to retreat until freedom had been won for all people in this great nation. For them, freedom and equality were truths worth fighting for.

Today God's truths are still worth fighting for, worth dying for. The men and women of the armed forces are willing to lay down their lives to protect this country, believing that freedom is worth dying for. The men and women who serve our community as protectors—firemen, policemen—also believe in a cause worth living and dying for. Many are dedicated to the truths that they see in God's Word, and so give their time, talent, and treasure, if not their lives, to spread righteousness across the globe, defend freedom, protect the innocent, and care for those in need.

We ought to bow our heads in thanks for those who have died to protect the freedoms we hold dear. We ought to say thank you to those who serve us every day to protect us from harm. We ourselves ought to hear the call of Christ to "be swift to answer Him" when we fight our daily battles against evil. God's truth never changes, nor should our resolve to stand for it, no matter what the cost.

Lead me in Your truth and teach me, for You are the God of my salvation; on You I wait all the day. PSALM 25:5

Jesus said to him, "I am the way, the truth, and the life. No one comes to the Father except through Me." JOHN 14:6

Then Peter opened his mouth and said: "In truth I perceive that God shows no partiality. But in every nation whoever fears Him and works righteousness is accepted by Him." ACTS 10:34, 35

There is neither Jew nor Greek, there is neither slave nor free, there is neither male nor female; for you are all one in Christ Jesus. GALATIANS 3:28

In Him you also trusted, after you heard the word of truth, the gospel of your salvation; in whom also, having believed, you were sealed with the Holy Spirit of promise, who is the guarantee of our inheritance until the redemption of the purchased possession, to the praise of His glory. EPHESIANS 1:13, 14

Glory! glory, hallelujah!

His truth is marching on.

Precious Savior,

Thank You for accepting me, for saving me, for setting me free, for drawing me to Yourself. Thank You for the truth of Your Word—truth on which I can stake my life. I trust in Your truth, and I praise You for making that truth known to me. Thank You that You are the way, the truth, and the life. Thank You for sealing me with Your promised Holy Spirit. Help me to discern lies from the truth and to always walk in Your truth. Amen.

Jesus Loves Me

Jesus loves me! this I know,

For the Bible tells me so.

Little ones to

They are weak, but He is strong

Anna B. Warner

1820-1915

REFLECTIONS

from Thomas Kinkade

It's the simplest tune. Easiest verse. Most difficult concept. "Jesus loves me, this I know, for the Bible tells me so." As I have taught these words to our four girls and seen their eyes dance with the delight of knowing their heavenly Father loves them, I marvel at the ease of their faith. Like almost all children, they take truth at face value. Understanding dependency comes intrinsically. I don't have to tell them to expect to see tomorrow, that they will always have something to eat at our table, or that I will always love them. They just know—because of experience, and because I've said so, and they trust me.

We would do well to learn from children in the area of faith. As we grow older, and in our own minds wiser, doubts creep into the picture of perfect love that was painted for us in our youth. Trials come, temptations arise, and we have the choice to believe that Jesus still loves us—or that He has changed His mind. It is at these moments that we must remember the simple words of this song and of the Scripture. God does love us, and He fills our lives with joy—regardless of the circumstances—because of His faithfulness. We can actually be excited about our faith, just like little children, because we know that we are always enveloped in our Abba's arms of grace.

In *Sunday Outing*, I tried to capture the innocence, excitement, and warmth that fills the hearts of all of God's children who trust Him to take care of them. It is a beautiful place in life to realize that we are chosen, favored, and wholly and dearly loved. The truth sets us free to celebrate Sunday—and every day—with our blessed Savior.

REMEMBER THE JOY

Jesus loves me! this I know,
For the Bible tells me so;
Little ones to Him belong,
They are weak, but He is strong.
Yes, Jesus loves me! Yes, Jesus loves me!
Yes, Jesus loves me! The Bible tells me so.

From mission fields across the planet to the Sunday school class down the hallway of a local church, this song is familiar to believers the world over. This is often the first song children learn in church—its simple melody and words about "little ones" who are "weak" resonates with them. Often it is the first song converts in foreign lands learn to sing about the basic truth of their newfound faith—Jesus loves me!

Jesus loves me. No other statement is so simple yet so fraught with depth of meaning. Who is Jesus? The Savior. God Himself. The Messiah. The One who came to earth as a tiny baby and grew up to die on the cross to take the punishment for our sins. The Bible is a big book with many difficult concepts and stories. We may find it difficult to understand all that the Bible teaches and to comprehend how it all fits together. But there is one fact that the Bible tells us clearly—Jesus loves us.

Jesus loves me! He who died
Heaven's gate to open wide;
He will wash away my sin,
Let His little child come in.
Yes, Jesus loves me! Yes, Jesus loves me!
Yes, Jesus loves me! The Bible tells me so.

This song was written by Anna Bartlett Warner in 1860. It was a poem included in a book written by Anna's sister Susan. The book Susan Warner wrote was called *Say and Seal*, and the poem was spoken by one of the characters in her story—a man who was comforting a dying child. As the man held the child, the child asked to hear a song. Instead of using one of the well-known songs of the day, Susan had her sister write a new one to include in her novel. Thus came this touching simple song of Jesus' love for His little children.

Anna and Susan Warner were the daughters of a prominent New York City lawyer. They had a home in the city, but their father purchased Constitution Island on the Hudson River to use as a retirement home. They had an uncle who worked at the United States Military Academy at West Point, right across the river from the island, and he urged the Warners' father to buy the piece of land. Their summer home was called "Good Crag," a portion of it dating back to the Revolutionary War, for the island had served as the connecting point for the chain that had protected the Hudson River from British invasion during the war for independence.

A depression in 1837 caused the loss of much of Mr. Warner's fortune, however, and the family went to live year-round on the island. Anna and Susan began writing in order to supplement the family income. Susan wrote several novels. One of them, *Wide, Wide World*, became second in sales and popularity only to Harriet Beecher Stowe's *Uncle Tom's Cabin*. Between them, the sisters wrote over one hundred publications. They summered on the island and wintered in the homes of friends on the mainland. Anna is known for a book called *Gardening by Myself* in which she put forth the radical idea that young women could do such things as dig in the dirt and plant gardens. Anna also published collections of verse. She and her sister published numerous works under pseudonyms as well.

To the military academy, however, they were probably best known for the Sunday school class that they taught to academy cadets for over forty years. Each week, West Point students would row across the Hudson River to the island. There, the sisters would serve lemonade and cookies and lead in singing and Bible study. Anna would write new hymns for the cadets to sing each week. After Anna wrote the text for "Jesus Loves Me" in 1860, the composer William Bradbury set it to music in 1861. Surely many cadets sang this simple song on those Sunday afternoons on the Hudson River. Susan died in 1885, but Anna continued the classes until her death in 1915. That year, one of her students was a young man named Dwight Eisenhower.

The two sisters are the only civilian women buried with military honors in the cemetery at the military academy. They earned the honor because of their dedication to the spiritual education of the cadets at West Point. The home, which is now a museum and is part of West Point, still holds many of the Warner family possessions.

Jesus loves me! He will stay
Close beside me all the way;
If I love Him, when I die
He will take me home on high.
Yes, Jesus loves me! Yes, Jesus loves me!
Yes, Jesus loves me! The Bible tells me so.

The entire Bible is the story of God's love. Jesus does indeed love us, and He promises to be close beside us throughout our lives. He created people out of His love.

The Bible that tells us about God's love also tells us that He loved people so much that He gave us the ability to choose to love Him or not. When Adam and Eve sinned, God immediately put into place a plan for salvation. Genesis 3:15 foreshadows that plan: "And I will put enmity between you and the woman, and between your seed and her Seed; He shall bruise your head, and you shall bruise His heel." The rest of the Bible tells the story of God's accomplishing that plan. He brought about a nation and a special family line into which He would send His Son.

The Bible tells us the story of why we need a Savior and what God has done about it. Sin brought death. Sin separated people from God, so God needed to deal with sin. He did so by taking the punishment Himself. He came to die for us. As He told His disciples, "Greater love has no one than this, than to lay down one's life for his friends" (John 15:13). There could be no greater definition of love than what Jesus did for us. There could be no greater love than His for us.

Yes indeed, Jesus loves you and me.

Little ones to Him belong.
They are weak.

But God demonstrates His own love toward us, in that while we were still sinners, Christ died for us. ROMANS 5:8

Who shall separate us from the love of Christ? Shall tribulation, or distress, or persecution, or famine, or nakedness, or peril, or sword? . . . Yet in all these things we are more than conquerors through Him who loved us. For I am persuaded that neither death nor life, nor angels nor principalities nor powers, nor things present nor things to come, nor height nor depth, nor any other created thing, shall be able to separate us from the love of God which is in Christ Jesus our Lord. ROMANS 8:35, 37–39

That Christ may dwell in your hearts through faith; that you, being rooted and grounded in love, may be able to comprehend with all the saints what is the width and length and depth and height—to know the love of Christ which passes knowledge; that you may be filled with all the fullness of God. EPHESIANS 3:17–19

God is love. In this the love of God was manifested toward us, that God has sent His only begotten Son into the world, that we might live through Him. In this is love, not that we loved God, but that He loved us and sent His Son to be the propitiation for our sins. 1 JOHN 4:8–10

but He is strong.

Dear Jesus,

You love me, this I know, because Your Word tells me so. I know that I belong to You because You are my Savior. No matter how weak I am, You will always be my strength. I know that You have washed away my sin so that I can come to You. Stay close beside me all the way. Because of all that You have done for me, help me to live for You.

Amen.

Joy to the World

Joy to the earth! the Savior reigns!

Let men their songs employ;

while fields and floods, rocks, hills,

Repeat the sounding joy.

Isaac Watts
1674-1748

REFLECTIONS

from Thomas Kinkade

THE HOPE OF HIS CALLING

They weren't exactly staying at the Crowne Plaza. Mary and Joseph, after enduring almost a year of speculation and judgment from others, coupled with all the normal challenges of pregnancy, now found themselves in a cold stable, awaiting the birth of their firstborn Son. Giving birth to the world's Savior probably wasn't how Mary imagined it would be. But God's plan never seemed to follow her course of logic. She had come to count on surprises and prayerfully pondered them in her heart, instead. She never knew what would come next, but she did know God's calling was on her life, and she was a firsthand witness to the miracles God makes in lives surrendered to Him.

Mary and Joseph had strength despite their difficult circumstances because they knew their calling: They were directly involved in God's plan of salvation. Each of us also has a part to play in God's plan of saving the earth for the sake of His kingdom. In God's economy, the size of the contribution matters little. What is important is that we remain true to those specific works for which God creatively and specifically fashioned us.

In *Silent Night*, I could feel the love and warmth that radiated from that solitary, lowly cottage as I painted it. Decked in lights, it gives off a glow in a dark, moonlit night, just as I imagine that first Christmas morn. One life or one home may not look like much. But when they are given fully into the Father's hands, the Master Carpenter begins an incredible work of art. Brick by brick, trial by trial, success by success, God fashions each piece into the image of His Son until just like the house, His light shines through us into a cold and dark world and whispers the hope found in Him. What joy has come to the world!

Joy to the world! the Lord is come!
Let earth receive her King;
Let every heart prepare Him room,
And heaven and nature sing,
And heaven and nature sing,
And heaven, and heaven and nature sing.

What does the word "joy" mean to you? You may think of the faces of your children, the wonder of your salvation, or the beauty of a sunset. Some moments are symbolic of what it means to experience joy.

However, joy can also be experienced in the middle of great difficulty. While we might not feel "happy" about some of our circumstances, we can still experience a deep, inner joy. Happiness is dependent upon our circumstances. When life is in order, when all is going smoothly, we are happy. Joy comes in spite of our circumstances because joy is not dependent upon how good we feel. We can experience joy even in times of pain and suffering, episodes of doubt and fear, circumstances of difficulty and trial. James wrote, "Count it all joy when you fall into various trials" (James 1:2). As He was facing the specter of the cross, Jesus told His disciples, "These things I have spoken to you, that My joy may remain in you, and that your joy may be full" (John 15:11).

Joy when we fall into trials? Joy when we face great difficulty? The Bible says a resounding yes! Joy can indeed be a reality in our lives. How can this be true? The Bible tells us that as well. David wrote in Psalm 16:11, "You will show me the path of life; in Your presence is fullness of joy; at Your right hand are pleasures forevermore." Quite simply, joy is found in God's presence. When we accept Jesus Christ as Savior and so come into a personal relationship with Him, we are given joy. The Holy Spirit comes into our lives and begins to grow His spiritual fruit in us—one of which is the fruit of joy (Gal. 5:22). The deep abiding joy that can carry us through even the darkest days is the joy found in the presence of Jesus.

How fitting, then, that a hymn about joy coming into the world is a hymn about Jesus coming into the world. When the earth receives her King and hearts prepare room for Him, then all heaven and nature can truly sing with joy.

This hymn was written by Isaac Watts, a man who has been called "the Father of English Hymnody." In his lifetime, he wrote over six hundred hymns, many published in 1707 in his hymnal, *Hymns and Spiritual Songs*. Many of his hymns were quite controversial because they were written, not directly with the words of the psalms in the Bible, but from his own heart (see the story of his early life in "When I Survey the Wondrous Cross," page 86).

In addition to writing hymns from the heart, however, Isaac did indeed rewrite all but twelve of the one hundred fifty psalms in the Bible (those twelve were psalms that he considered unfit for worship). These were published in 1719 in the hymnal, *The Psalms of David*. In Watts' day, congregational singing in the church was very dreary and difficult. When Isaac was just a teenager, he became frustrated with the singing in church and was challenged to write something better. He began to paraphrase the psalms so that they would be more understandable to the congregation, thus giving more meaning to the people's singing and worship.

The famous hymn "Joy to the World" came from Isaac Watts' paraphrase of Psalm 98. "Shout joyfully to the LORD, all the earth; break forth in song, rejoice, and sing praises. . . . Shout joyfully before the LORD, the King" (Ps. 98:4, 6).

It is unknown whether Isaac Watts was thinking of this as a Christmas hymn when he wrote it, but it has certainly become one

of the most beloved hymns of the season. It resonates Christmas, for it speaks of the joy that came into the world when the Savior, the King, came from heaven to earth as a tiny baby in a manger. That tiny child would change the world forever. No wonder heaven and nature sing!

Joy to the earth! the Savior reigns!
Let men their songs employ;
While fields and floods, rocks, hills, and plains
Repeat the sounding joy, repeat the sounding joy,
Repeat, repeat the sounding joy.

Psalm 98 tells of the songs of people mingling with the songs of nature: "Sing to the LORD with the harp, with the harp and the sound of a psalm. . . . Let the sea roar, and all its fullness, the world and those who dwell in it; let the rivers clap their hands; let the hills be joyful together before the LORD" (Ps. 98:5, 7, 8).

Yes, there is joy in the world. The earth itself sings as the wind blows through the fields, the water rushes down the stream, the rocks, hills, and plains join with their own particular song. When Christ the Savior came, He brought joy to the earth. He brought His presence that would stay with His people through His Holy Spirit.

No more let sins and sorrows grow,
Nor thorns infest the ground;
He comes to make His blessings flow
Far as the curse is found, far as the curse is found,
Far as, far as the curse is found.

The Savior brought joy to the world because by His life and death, He renews all of creation. And one day, He will come again to rule, forever overturning the curse that sin brought both into creation and into the hearts of all people. Adam and Eve sinned and had to leave the Garden of Eden, sent out into the wilderness where thorns would grow in the fields they tried to plant and harvest. Sin had made its mark on all of creation. The curse infected everything. But Jesus came to make His blessings flow across a cursed earth and to bring His joy. So even in times of great difficulty and struggle, His joy can be known. The curse still exists, but Jesus' blood on the cross enables us to experience deep abiding joy no matter what our circumstances.

He rules the world with truth and grace,
And makes the nations prove
The glories of His righteousness,
And wonders of His love, and wonders of His love,
And wonders, wonders of His love.

"For He is coming to judge the earth. With righteousness He shall judge the world, and the peoples with equity" (Ps. 98:9). The curse of sin is not permanent. Christ will come to judge the earth. Even now, He rules in the hearts of His people, bringing the light of His truth and grace into a dark and sinful world.

At Christmas, believers all over the world praise God for sending His Son and bringing the reality of joy into our lives. Indeed, when the angel spoke to the shepherds about the birth of this very special baby, he said, "Do not be afraid, for behold, I bring

Let every heart

you good tidings of great joy which will be to all people. For there is born to you this day in the city of David a Savior, who is Christ the Lord" (Luke 2:10, 11). The song focuses on the Lord who has come to be King of our lives and, one day, King of a new creation. The song reminds us of the wonders of such love—the love of a God who would take the curse upon Himself so that we might experience joy.

Joy to the world! The Lord is come!

But let all those rejoice who put their trust in You; let them ever shout for joy, because You defend them; let those also who love Your name be joyful in You. PSALM 5:11

"Until now you have asked nothing in My name. Ask, and you will receive, that your joy may be full." JOHN 16:24

For the kingdom of God is not eating and drinking, but righteousness and peace and joy in the Holy Spirit. ROMANS 14:17

Therefore we also, since we are surrounded by so great a cloud of witnesses, let us lay aside every weight, and the sin which so easily ensnares us, and let us run with endurance the race that is set before us, looking unto Jesus, the author and finisher of our faith, who for the joy that was set before Him endured the cross, despising the shame, and has sat down at the right hand of the throne of God. HEBREWS 12:1, 2

prepare Him room.

Dear Lord,

Thank You for coming to earth. Thank You for bringing joy to the world! I praise You for offering me that same joy through Your Holy Spirit. Grow the fruit of joy in me. May I experience the deep abiding joy that stays within no matter what circumstances I face. Let me, along with all of Your creation, repeat the sounding joy of Your presence in my life.

Amen.

All the Way My Savior Leads Me

When my spirit, clothed immortal,

wings its flight to realms of day,

This my song through e...

Jesus led me all the way.

Fanny J. Crosby
1820-1915

REFLECTIONS

from Thomas Kinkade

It seemed an incredible risk. Everything Nanette and I loved about our home in Placerville—the rural, quiet, and unpretentious setting—would go by the wayside if we procceded with plans to move to the much more expensive and industrial Silicon Valley.

Yet we both felt we heard God's calling. If we were to grow the business, we had to be more centrally located to the people interested in our industry. So we began to pray.

It wasn't long before God swung open wide the door that led us right into the perfect location. We kept praying for a studio, and soon our next-door neighbor, who had lived in her home for over 35 years, decided she had found another home she liked better. She sold us her cottage—an ideal work situation for me and my family. The same kind of scenario happened when we asked God whether or not I should expand from producing only originals to print work, as well. He answered, "Yes," and the blessings keep coming.

It astounds me how intimately acquainted Jesus is with all our ways. He knows when we sit down and

THE DOOR TO ADVENTURE

when we rise up, and He even perceives our thoughts from afar. Greater still, He knows what the future holds. Who better than my loving Father can give me the direction I need in life? I simply trust His guidance and walk forward in faith—submitting to closed doors and walking through the open ones.

Of course, it's not always easy. The unexpected can be frightening, and I think a lot of us feel fearful that He'll deny us what we really secretly want if we obey Him completely. The truth, though, is that He loves us more than we can know and longs to lavish on us the delights of life that bring true happiness. Life with Christ at the lead is an amazing adventure, full of thrills, joy, and rewards that we can enjoy both now and in the life to come.

All the way my Savior leads me—
What have I to ask beside?
Can I doubt His tender mercy,
Who through life has been my guide?
Heavenly peace, divinest comfort,
Here by faith in Him to dwell!
For I know, whate'er befall me,
Jesus doeth all things well.

Life is often compared to a road. We walk along that road through the years of our lives, unable to see too far into the distance, not knowing what may meet us around the curve ahead. We travel—sometimes walking with friends and family, sometimes alone.

We'd all like to have a map of our lives. Here we are at point A; there is our hoped-for final end at point B. Those who are believers have their sights set on the city of God—heaven—as did Pilgrim on his journey in *Pilgrim's Progress*. In the meantime, of course, we have a long road to walk. We have desires, dreams, destinations. We have goals and hopes. So we begin to map out a course for our lives. Some may map the logical routes; others might take the roads less traveled. However, we would do well to always hold our life maps loosely. We may set our goals, lay out our courses, and map our lives, but when it is all said and done, God is ultimately overseeing it all. We are far better off when we recognize that, surrender our lives to Him, and then make our plans and take our walk *with* Him. That means being flexible and allowing Him to change the course at times instead of constantly trying to go our own way.

You see, God has the master map. He sees our entire pathway from start to finish. He knows what dangers lurk ahead. He knows about the scenic rest spots along the way. He has reasons for taking

us at times on the circuitous route instead of through shortcuts, across rugged terrain instead of pleasant valleys. The Bible tells us, "For I know the thoughts that I think toward you, says the LORD, thoughts of peace and not of evil, to give you a future and a hope" (Jer. 29:11). The pathway the Lord has laid out for us on His master map is a pathway perfect for us. He has a future and a hope planned. He does not promise that the path will always be easy. He does promise, however, to lead us "all the way."

When Fanny Crosby wrote this hymn, she had many years of the Savior's guidance behind her. She was born on March 24, 1820, in New York. Like any parents, hers surely had great plans for her—the beginning of a map for little Fanny's life. But the route quickly changed. When Fanny was just six weeks old, she experienced inflammation in her eyes that was improperly treated, resulting in blindness. The lights went out on the small child, but not the light in her heart. She was an optimistic person and grew up like any child, playing and enjoying life and friends. She refused to let her blindness be a hindrance to herself or to her family. God was taking her on a different route, and she followed Him gladly. As she looked back over the years of her life, Fanny understood that she could not doubt her Savior's "tender mercy," for she had experienced it from her Guide. She could say with conviction, "I know, whate'er befall me, Jesus doeth all things well."

All the way my Savior leads me—
Cheers each winding path I tread,
Gives me grace for every trial,
Feeds me with the living bread.
Though my weary steps may falter,
And my soul athirst may be,
Gushing from the Rock before me,
Lo! a spring of joy I see.

When she was five years old, Fanny went to New York City to be checked by doctors there, only to discover that the blindness was incurable. When she was eleven, the first school for the blind was opened in the United States, in New York City. Fanny arrived at the New York Institute for the Blind just before she turned fifteen, and there she received her education. Lessons were given by readings and lectures, for this was fifteen years before Braille was invented and put into use. Fanny had a keen mind and a wonderful memory, however. She had been listening to Bible stories, great literature, and poetry since she was a child, resulting in an intense desire for knowledge and literature.

When she was twenty-two, she was appointed to be a teacher at the school. She also became recognized as the poet laureate of the institution, often composing poems for distinguished visitors or for special occasions. In 1844, a collection of her poems was published in a work entitled *The Blind Girl and Other Poems*. Other books followed. She was involved with other teachers and pupils in going to exhibitions to advertise the school, as well as even saying a poem in front of a joint session of Congress in a visit to interest the government in education for the blind. One coworker who served as secretary of the institution was a man named Grover Cleveland. Long before he became president, he had copied down many of Fanny Crosby's poems for her. She became very well known in New York as the "hymn queen." In 1858, she married a blind music teacher at the institute, Alexander Van Alstyne.

Fanny Crosby could have lived her life in bitterness and anger at the pathway she had been forced to tread. She chose instead to follow her Savior's lead. By that choice, she walked with the One who cheered her along the "winding path" and gave her "grace for every trial." Surely there were days of frustration and situations of embarrassment, but in the times when her "weary steps" would falter or her soul would experience thirst, Jesus was right there with a "spring of joy" for her to drink and find refreshment.

All the way my Savior leads me—
O the fullness of His love!
Perfect rest to me is promised
In my Father's house above.
When my spirit, clothed immortal,
Wings its flight to realms of day,
This my song through endless ages:
Jesus led me all the way.

Fanny Crosby wrote over six thousand hymns during her lifetime. In her early days, she wrote secular verse that became very popular. It wasn't until her early forties that she began to write gospel song lyrics as she teamed up with church musicians such as W. B. Bradbury, Dr. Robert Lowry, and Ira Sankey (the musician who traveled with Dwight Moody). It is said that she never wrote a text without first asking her Savior to lead her. Thanks to her wonderful memory, she would often compose an entire hymn—or a few at a time—and then dictate the words to a secretary.

The simple story behind this hymn is that she received a direct answer to prayer. She was in desperate need of five dollars and did not know how she would get it. So she prayed for God's provision. Within moments a knock came at the door and a stranger gave her five dollars. She said that her first thought was to thank the Lord for the wonderful way in which He lead her. The poem was written, Dr. Lowry set it to music (as he did with the hymn, "I Need Thee Every Hour," page 38), and this popular hymn was born.

It is said that at one time in her life, a preacher sympathetically remarked that he wished the Lord had given Fanny her sight. Her reply surprised him. She quickly responded that if she had been able to ask for one thing at birth, she would have asked for blindness. Her reason? "Because when I get to heaven, the first face that shall ever gladden my sight will be that of my Savior!"

Life will surprise us with twists and turns. Sometimes the path is through breezy valleys; at other times we must struggle across rocky mountains or through dark forests. What will be our song as we go? Will we complain and be angry that the path is not as we wanted or planned? Or can we walk calmly beside the One who holds the map? Wherever your path leads today, sing with Fanny Crosby,

This my song through endless ages: Jesus led me all the way.

You will show me the path of life; in Your presence is fullness of joy; at Your right hand are pleasures forevermore. PSALM 16:11

For this is God, our God forever and ever; He will be our guide even to death. PSALM 48:14

You know my sitting down and my rising up; You understand my thought afar off. You comprehend my path and my lying down, and are acquainted with all my ways. . . . In Your book they all were written, the days fashioned for me, when as yet there were none of them. PSALM 139:2, 3, 16

For as many as are led by the Spirit of God, these are sons of God. ROMANS 8:14

For the Lamb who is in the midst of the throne will shepherd them and lead them to living fountains of waters. And God will wipe away every tear from their eyes. REVELATION 7:17

Jesus led me all the way.

My Savior,

I know that You already know the pathway of my life—and I know that at times I fight against You. I often want to go my own way, take a shortcut, avoid the difficult terrain. Help me to follow You, Lord. I need not doubt Your tender mercy, Your comfort, Your cheer. I know that Your plans for me are for good and not for evil, to give me a future and a hope. Jesus, lead me all the way. Amen.

When I Survey the Wondrous Cross

Were the whole realm of nature mine,

That were a present far too small;

Love so amazing,

Demands my soul, my life, my all.

Isaac Watts
1674-1748

REFLECTIONS
from Thomas Kinkade

Looking back over the past few years, decades, even centuries, I couldn't escape the sense of darkness that I felt enshrouded this past millennium. It was time for a new beginning, a rebirth into the light and love of Christ. Out of this passion and expectation, *Sunrise* was born—my attempt to convey the sense of destiny our new millennium holds for believers across the globe.

It may seem odd to depict such a classic symbol of the past to herald a brighter future, but the cross—and its inherent symbolism—is the only way to bridge the divide. Standing tall and sure against the glorious light above, Christ's resolve, dedication, and love is shown as a universal embrace of the creation below. A small vine trickles down symbolizing the beginning of new life that stems from Christ's death. And from the hill to the horizon, countless mountain ranges and valleys undulate beneath the power of the cross—a graphic depiction of our lives as we travel through life not in a straight line, but up, down, under, and around life's triumphs and challenges until we reach our hope's final destination. Even the wisps of fog among the peaks point to our own frailty, our lives existing only for a moment in time, and then on to eternity.

I anticipate this new era to be the millennium of light—a time when eyes will be opened, hearts cleansed, and hope begun anew as we realize the incredible work Christ finished for us on that blessed cross. Then we will release our grip on this world and lay it as a crown at Jesus feet, only to see that the most spectacular works pale in comparison to the radiance and richness of the love He has shown us.

MILLENNIUM OF LIGHT

When I survey the wondrous cross
On which the Prince of Glory died,
My richest gain I count but loss,
And pour contempt on all my pride.

Forbid it, Lord, that I should boast,
Save in the death of Christ my God;
All the vain things that charm me most,
I sacrifice them to His blood.

The cross. We wear it around our necks as jewelry. We see it on the tops of churches or on the front of Bibles. Stainless steel, diamond-encrusted, or brass-inlaid crosses—truly things of beauty.

In reality, however, the cross was an instrument of horror. The Romans invented the spectacle of crucifixion for their worst criminals who were nailed or tied to wooden crosses and set up in public places in order to teach an unmistakable lesson to the rest of the population. Crosses were not a thing of beauty in the Roman Empire—no one wanted to wear a duplicate as jewelry.

For believers, however, the cross has indeed become a thing of beauty. Two thousand years ago a seemingly insignificant man was crucified on a Roman cross. That man was the Son of God who died a cruel death in order to bring salvation to our entire planet—with His blood covering all sin from the beginning of time until its end. His outstretched arms encompassed a hopeless world and brought assurance of salvation to all who believe. Believers who "survey the wondrous cross" on which their Savior died begin to understand the cross's beauty. The cross defeated sin and death. The cross bridged the chasm between sinful humanity and the holy God. The cross brings us into a relationship with Him.

The cross also puts our humanity into perspective. No matter what gains we might achieve during our time on this earth, no matter how proud we may be of our accomplishments, all are of little value when we survey the wondrous cross and understand that through it alone we have been offered eternal life.

As Paul wrote to the Galatians, "But God forbid that I should boast except in the cross of our Lord Jesus Christ, by whom the world has been crucified to me, and I to the world" (Gal. 6:14). Nothing is as important as Jesus.

The author of this hymn was Isaac Watts. He was born on July 7, 1674, in Southhampton, England. He was the oldest of eight children in a family caught in the difficult days of persecution of those in England who sought to worship God as they chose. His was a godly family; however, Isaac's father was labeled a "Dissenter" because he did not adhere to the established order and doctrine of the Church of England. Isaac's father was imprisoned during the time Isaac was born.

Isaac was a very precocious child—by age thirteen he had learned Latin, Greek, French, and Hebrew, and he could write good poetry. He even developed the somewhat annoying habit of often speaking in rhyme! He was offered an education at Oxford or Cambridge but could not attend unless he would renounce his religious convictions. He refused. As a result, he went to an institution called the Dissenting Academy run by independent believers for those who were barred from the main universities. Over the years he would write books on many topics including catechisms for children, astronomy, metaphysics, and even a popular book of children's poetry.

Although one hundred fifty years before, Martin Luther had mainstreamed the singing of hymns in many churches, there were many more congregations for whom hymn singing had not yet become the norm. Most of the singing in the churches was taken

directly from the Psalms, resulting in ponderous, dreary music. At one point, Watts could stand it no longer. His complaint resulted in a challenge for him to write something better. He took the challenge.

Isaac Watts would write over six hundred hymns. His goal was merely to update the Psalms, making them easier to sing and bringing out their deep meaning so that Christians could worship wholeheartedly. Many Christians of the day, however, considered his renditions to be too worldly—he outraged many, and some churches even split over the use of his music.

In 1702, Watts was ordained as pastor of an independent congregation, a position he held for the rest of his life. In spite of lifelong health problems, he was a beloved pastor and distinguished theologian. In 1707, Watts published his first book of hymns, titled simply, *Hymns and Spiritual Songs*. Another book of hymns called *The Psalms of David* was published in 1719. Some hymns from his pen inspired by psalms include: "Jesus Shall Reign Where'er the Sun" (Psalm 72); "O God, Our Help in Ages Past" (Psalm 90); and "Joy to the World" (Psalm 98). Fellow believers and hymn writers John and Charles Wesley also recognized his genius. When they published their book of hymns, they included many hymns belonging to Isaac Watts.

The hymn "When I Survey the Wondrous Cross" was extremely controversial in its day. It came not directly from a psalm, but instead was written solely from his heart and was based on his personal feelings about what Christ had done.

See, from His head, His hands, His feet,
Sorrow and love flow mingled down;
Did e'er such love and sorrow meet,
Or thorns compose so rich a crown?

Watts took the picture of Christ's crucifixion from Scripture and painted himself into the story. He looked at his beloved Savior with His hands and feet nailed to the cruel cross. On His head was the crown of thorns, pressed into His brow. Blood flowed freely from the wounds, mixed with sorrow and love—sorrow over sin, love for the sinners for whom He was giving His life.

At that moment, Christ was transforming the rugged cross into the instrument of complete forgiveness. He was transforming a circle of thorns into a kingly crown.

Were the whole realm of nature mine,
That were a present far too small;
Love so amazing, so divine,
Demands my soul, my life, my all.

This song encapsulates our faith. It helps us understand the depths of God's love for us that He would send His Son not as a king, but as a lowly child in a manger. He came not to receive honor and great glory, but to die the death of a despised thief. Why did He do it? To give us salvation. To bring us back to Himself.

What a gift! We have nothing to which to cling except the love of God shown so clearly by His shed blood on the cross. There is nothing we can give in return. Even if we owned all of nature, it would be too small a gift. Love so amazing, so divine, that it gives its life for us is love that demands our souls, our lives, our all.

For the message of the cross is foolishness to those who are perishing, but to us who are being saved it is the power of God.
1 CORINTHIANS 1:18

Yet indeed I also count all things loss for the excellence of the knowledge of Christ Jesus my Lord, for whom I have suffered the loss of all things, and count them as rubbish, that I may gain Christ and be found in Him, not having my own righteousness, which is from the law, but that which is through faith in Christ, the righteousness which is from God by faith; that I may know Him and the power of His resurrection, and the fellowship of His sufferings, being conformed to His death.
PHILIPPIANS 3:8–10

Therefore we also, since we are surrounded by so great a cloud of witnesses, let us lay aside every weight, and the sin which so easily ensnares us, and let us run with endurance the race that is set before us, looking unto Jesus, the author and finisher of our faith, who for the joy that was set before Him endured the cross, despising the shame, and has sat down at the right hand of the throne of God. HEBREWS 12:1, 2

Who Himself bore our sins in His own body on the tree, that we, having died to sins, might live for righteousness—by whose stripes you were healed. 1 PETER 2:24

my soul, my life, my all.

Dearest Lord Jesus,

Thank You that You left Your glory above to come to earth and take up the cross on which You shed Your blood for me. May I never take for granted the depth of Your love for me, shown so clearly on the day that Your sorrow and love mingled with Your blood in order to bring me back to You. Help me always to remember that nothing I have or gain on this earth has any value compared to what You have prepared for me in eternity. Help me to be willing to daily give You my soul, my life, my all.

Amen.

Softly and Tenderly

Will L. Thompson, 1847-1909

1. Soft - ly and ten - der
2. Why should we tar
3. Time is now flee
4. Oh! for the wo

Come home, come home,

Ye who are weary, come home;

Earnestly, tenderly, Je

Calling, "O sinner, come home!

Will L. Thompson
1847-1909

REFLECTIONS

from Thomas Kinkade

My father was 83 years old when I held his hand for the last time. It was a few weeks before Christmas, and my brother and sister and I gathered around his bedside. I asked, "Dad, do you know Jesus loves you?" He answered, "Yes, my son." "Are you ready to see Him? It won't be long, now." His reply was the assurance: "I am ready to go." I knew he was. He had surrendered his life to Christ several years earlier.

Suddenly, his spirit was gone, leaving behind a weary, withered, old body he wouldn't need anymore. He had walked up the steps to glory and had embraced a new life, a new body, and a new hope right before my very eyes. What amazing mercy God extended to me to watch that process firsthand, to witness the glorious exchange of pained, broken, and imperfect life for that which is whole, holy, and eternal.

Losing someone is never easy. But for Christians, the transition from death to life holds such incredible hope and promise that we can embrace it as a walkway to a reunion. It's the image that I tried to convey in *Stairway to Paradise,* where the process leads us to a new Garden of Eden, a new beginning where we once again commune unhindered with the Father. While we don't know exactly what lies at the top of the stairs (for the Bible says we can now only see as in a mirror dimly), we know it will be better than our wildest imaginations. The same God that created this beautiful world we live in has long been at work preparing a place just for us. He has called us and wooed us our whole lives long. At last, we will enter His rest and rejoice in the unveiling of His final masterpiece, our home with Him in heaven.

THE GREAT EXCHANGE

Softly and tenderly Jesus is calling,
Calling for you and for me;
See, on the portals He's waiting and watching,
Watching for you and for me.
Come home, come home,
Ye who are weary, come home;
Earnestly, tenderly, Jesus is calling,
Calling, "O sinner, come home!"

Where is your home? What do you think of when you hear the word "home"? Perhaps you consider your own plot of land where you hang your hat, kiss your spouse, and hug your kids. Maybe it's a quiet, restful place where you live alone. Perhaps your thoughts go back to the home of your past, where you played and fought with brothers and sisters, where you learned to ride a bike, where you opened Christmas presents.

Or maybe your thoughts send you to your grandparents' home—sweet memories of warm cookies and an elderly person's hands, always ready to grasp yours.

Perhaps the word "home" doesn't engender warm memories. If yours was broken or scarred, the memories of home don't mean that much to you at all.

So what does Jesus mean when He softly and tenderly calls us to "come home"? When we come home to Jesus, we come to the place of greatest joy, comfort, love, and peace that we could ever know. Nothing on earth, no matter how good, can compare to our home with God. When we come home to Jesus, we find forgiveness for our sin and a relationship with the Father, the God who created us. When we come home to Jesus, we are truly home.

Jesus is calling, tenderly calling, desiring that we would heed the sense of discontent and frustration we feel, understanding that this sense of uncertainty is because we are not "home." So He calls. He doesn't push His way into our lives, dragging us kicking and screaming to a place where we don't want to go. No, He is waiting and watching, looking down the road for the next weary traveler who wants to come home.

Jesus called to His disciples. Standing on the beach, He spoke to the burly men on the fishing boat, saying, "Follow Me, and I will make you fishers of men" (Matt. 4:19). When they came to Jesus, they found, as Peter said, "the Christ, the Son of the living God" (John 6:69). When asked if he would go away, Peter replied, "Lord, to whom shall we go? You have the words of eternal life" (John 6:68). Peter knew that with Christ, he was home.

Jesus called the woman who touched His cloak and so experienced healing to come forward. He knew who she was, but He wanted her to identify herself and so receive His words, "Daughter, be of good cheer; your faith has made you well. Go in peace" (Luke 8:48). She had discovered faith and so had come home.

He called a young girl to arise from the dead. He called Lazarus out of the tomb. Both returned from the grave to life on earth—a blessing to those who had been left behind and a promise of joy for the certainty of their future home in heaven.

He called Zacchaeus the tax collector down out of his perch in the tree. With great joy, Zacchaeus brought the Savior home and his life changed from that day. "And Jesus said to him, 'Today salvation has come to this house, because he also is a son of Abraham; for the Son of Man has come to seek and to save that which was lost'" (Luke 19:9, 10). Jesus seeks and saves the lost and brings them home.

He came, not to save those who think themselves righteous, but those who know they are sinners. "Those who are well have no need of a physician, but those who are sick. I did not come to call the righteous, but sinners, to repentance" (Mark 2:17).

Softly and tenderly, Jesus is still calling, "O sinner, come home."

Why should we tarry when Jesus is pleading,
Pleading for you and for me?
Why should we linger and heed not His mercies,
Mercies for you and for me?

At some point in his life, Will L. Thompson heard the call of Jesus. Born on November 7, 1847, in East Liverpool, Ohio, Thompson was a music lover for life. He attended the Boston Music School from 1870 to 1873, later doing additional study in Germany. He had always wanted to write music and had a very successful career writing secular songs before he turned to gospel music. He began his own music publishing and music store business with branches in East Liverpool and in Chicago, where he got to know D. L. Moody (founder of Moody Bible Institute, located in Chicago). Moody used this hymn, "Softly and Tenderly," as an invitation hymn in the evangelistic meetings he and his coworker, Ira Sankey, held in the United States and Great Britain. It is said that on his deathbed, Moody told Thompson, "Will, I would rather have written 'Softly and Tenderly' than anything I have been able to do in my whole life."

Time is now fleeting, the moments are passing,
Passing from you and from me;
Shadows are gathering, deathbeds are coming,
Coming for you and for me.

As an invitation hymn, the words call to those who think that they don't yet need Christ, don't yet want to make the commitment, don't yet want to think about the possibility of death and its aftermath. The song calls us not to tarry, for Jesus is pleading. He knows the time is short; He wants us to accept His mercies—for this life *and* for the life to come.

O for the wonderful love He has promised,
Promised for you and for me;
Though we have sinned He has mercy and pardon,
Pardon for you and for me.

Do you hear Jesus calling? You will if you still your heart and listen closely. You may hear Him calling from the long-ago prayers you heard your parents or grandparents praying for you. You may hear Him calling from a long-ago commitment that you failed to follow through on and had forgotten. He may be calling you from the pulpit of the church you attend sporadically or only methodically. He may be calling through the eyes of your young children as they snuggle into your arms. You may hear Him in pain and suffering or in moments of overwhelming joy.

He's calling.

Come home, come home,
Ye who are weary, come home;
Earnestly, tenderly, Jesus is calling,
Calling, "O sinner, come home!"

Are you weary? Come home. Do you need rest? Come home. Do you desperately desire a place of love, forgiveness, and peace? Come home.

Jesus is calling. Come home.

Ye who

"I will arise and go to my father, and will say to him, 'Father, I have sinned against heaven and before you, and I am no longer worthy to be called your son. Make me like one of your hired servants.' And he arose and came to his father. But when he was still a great way off, his father saw him and had compassion, and ran and fell on his neck and kissed him. And the son said to him, 'Father, I have sinned against heaven and in your sight, and am no longer worthy to be called your son.' But the father said to his servants, 'Bring out the best robe and put it on him, and put a ring on his hand and sandals on his feet. And bring the fatted calf here and kill it, and let us eat and be merry; for this my son was dead and is alive again; he was lost and is found.' " LUKE 15:18–24

"Behold, I stand at the door and knock. If anyone hears My voice and opens the door, I will come in to him and dine with him, and he with Me." REVELATION 3:20

See, on the portals
He's waiting and watching.
Watching for you and for me.

are weary, come home.

My Jesus,

I hear You calling. I know that You are softly and tenderly calling me to come home. I want to come home, Lord. I want to come home to You. Thank You for accepting me, a sinner who needs Your forgiveness. Thank You for promising mercy and pardon.   *Amen.*